CW00341073

ZELENSKY

First published by
Alfabet Uitgevers, The Netherlands in 2022.
Published by Canbury Press 2022
This edition published 2022

Canbury Press
Kingston upon Thames, Surrey, United Kingdom
www.canburypress.com

Printed and bound in Great Britain
by CPI Group (UK) Ltd, Croydon
Cover: Daniel Benneworth-Gray

This publication has been made possible with financial support from the
Dutch Foundation for Literature

Nederlands
letterenfonds
dutch foundation
for literature

This is a work of non-fiction

FSC
www.fsc.org
MIX
Paper from
responsible sources
FSC® C171272

FSC® helps take care of forests for future generations.

ISBN
Hardback: 9781912454778
Ebook: 9781912454785

ZELENSKY

Ukraine's President and His Country

**Steven Derix and
Marina Shelkunova**

Translated by Brent Annable

Contents

Introduction

Vladimir Putin rarely underestimates his opponent. At the KGB Academy in Leningrad, he learned the meticulous art of profiling 'targets' of the service, whether they were Russian dissidents or East German Communist apparatchiks.

Before meeting with anybody, Putin first analyses their strengths and weaknesses. During his first visit to the United States, he wound President George W. Bush around his little finger, with pious tales of his christening in the Russian Orthodox Church. Afterwards, an obviously charmed Bush told of how he had looked into the 'soul' of the former KGB officer. When German Chancellor Angela Merkel visited Sochi in 2007 to discuss energy policy, Putin had his black labrador Konni brought in. Merkel – who is terrified of dogs – dared not budge an inch, and Putin dominated the conversation.

Vladimir Putin also carefully considers way he talks *about* people. The Russian President is only too aware of the political appeal of Alexey Navalny, and will therefore never allow the name of the opposition leader to cross his lips – not even since Navalny's incarceration in January 2021. Putin's spokesperson, Dmitri Peskov, consistently refers to Navalny as 'that blogger.'

In April 2019, Volodymyr Zelensky was elected as the sixth President of Ukraine, with nearly three-quarters of the vote.

One month later, the Russian President attended the World Economic Forum in St. Petersburg. It had been five years since Russia's annexation of Crimea but daily skirmishes between the Ukrainian army and pro-Russian separatists were still commonplace in eastern Ukraine.

'Why did you not congratulate Volodymyr Zelenksy when he became President?' asked the interviewer.

Putin breathed a heavy sigh. The Russian officials and business magnates in the room playfully nudged one another: this was going to be good.

'You know,' said Putin, 'he is still pushing a certain rhetoric. He labels us "enemies" and "aggressors." Perhaps he should think about what he really wants to achieve, what he wants to do.'

Putin had still not once uttered the name 'Zelensky.'

'You are the President of a world power,' the interviewer fawned, 'and right now, he is incredibly popular in his country. Both of you could start with a clean slate. Even a small gesture might completely change the course of world history. Why not simply arrange a meeting?'

'Playing the President': *Volodymyr Zelensky, formerly an actor, became Ukraine's President in May 2019.* Ukraine Government

Putin gave the enormous hall an almost pitying look, and waited until the sniggering from the officials and businesspeople had died down.

'Did I say "no"?' replied Putin. With a snide grin, he added: 'Nobody has invited me.'

'Are you prepared to meet with him?'

Putin now looked genuinely amused. 'Listen, I do not know this man. I hope that we can meet one day. As far as I can tell, he's amazing at what he does, he's a marvellous actor.'

Laughter and generous applause filled the room.

Putin continued: 'But seriously: it's one thing to play a person, but quite another thing to be that person.'

The blue-suited officials knew exactly what Putin meant. The Ukrainian President had started his career as a comic actor and comedian. From 2015-2019, Zelensky was the star of the Ukrainian hit series *Servant of the People*. He played history teacher Vasyl Holoborodko, who after a long day of teaching launches into a tirade against all of the injustices in Ukraine: corruption, broken election promises, stagnation and poverty, and the tax privileges, *dachas,* and motorcycle escorts enjoyed by the political class.

A student secretly films Holoborodko's damning speech, and puts the video online. The tirade goes viral, and the young history teacher – who still lives with his parents – is invited to go into politics. He wins with a landslide victory, becoming the first ever Ukrainian head of state who cycles to work. Holoborodko turns the political world upside-down, steering the country towards a glorious future. The series tapped into a classic populist theme, that of the political outsider who makes short work of the 'old regime.' In 2019, the final season of *Servant of the People* blended seamlessly into a slick election campaign for the soon-to-be President. Servant of the People (*Sluha Narodu*) became the name of Zelensky's political party, which won an absolute majority later that year in the Ukrainian parliament, the *Verkhovna Rada*.

Putin was right about one thing: until that time, Zelensky had only ever played the President.

The former showman was now placed at the helm of a bankrupt country – a nation at war with a political and administrative system that was corrupt to the core. In the 30 years of independence since the disintegration of the Soviet Union, Ukraine had been unable to disentangle itself from the chaos that gripped the country in 1991. Zelensky promised to solve all the problems within a single, five-year term.

Many thought that he would fail. Within months of his election, Zelensky's reform programme had ground to a halt, resulting in a life-and-death battle with the all-powerful oligarchs. To survive within the Ukrainian *House of Cards*, Zelensky resorted to unconventional means. Human rights organisations expressed concern for his autocratic tendencies. Ukrainian patriots feared that the new President would sell out Crimea and the Donbas to secure peace with Moscow. The Public Prosecutor's Office in the Netherlands was outraged when Zelensky exchanged a key witness with Russia during the investigation into the shooting down of the Malaysian Airlines flight MH17 over Ukraine in 2014.

In September 2019, Zelensky became unwittingly embroiled in a scandal surrounding the potential abuse of powers by the American President, Donald Trump.

During a telephone conversation on 25th July, Trump supposedly put pressure on Zelensky to launch a criminal investigation against Trump's opponent in the imminent presidential elections, Joe Biden. According to unfounded rumours circulating in Trumpland, while working as Vice-

President under Barack Obama, Biden had insisted on the dismissal of Ukraine's Prosecutor, General Viktor Shokin, in order to suppress an investigation into his son, Hunter Biden and his employer, the Ukrainian gas company Burisma.

During his telephone conversation with Zelensky, Trump denied any wrongdoing. As proof, the White House published a transcript of the conversation between the two Presidents.

Zelensky came across as a spineless sycophant. 'We are trying to work hard because we wanted to drain the swamp here in our country,' the Ukrainian President said, parroting Trump's own election slogan. 'We brought in many, many new people. Not the old politicians, not the typical politicians, because we want to have a new format and a new type of government. You are a great teacher for us.'

The Russian state television service – under the Kremlin's control – branded Zelensky a clown. In the summer of 2021, during a major press conference held for the Russian people (broadcast under the title of *A Direct Line with Vladimir Putin*), Putin was asked whether he would now be prepared to meet with Zelensky. Putin replied that it would be of no use whatsoever, since Zelensky had 'placed the governance of his country squarely in international hands. It is not Kyiv that calls the shots in Ukraine, but Washington.'

It is altogether possible that Putin really believed what he said.

On 24th February 2022, Putin launched a large-scale invasion of Ukraine. While Russian troops attacked on four fronts, tanks advanced on Kyiv. Once Zelensky and his government were eradicated, the rest of Ukraine would quickly fall back in line with Russia – or so the Kremlin thought.

But Putin's Blitzkrieg proved to be a misstep. After a month of fighting, many Russian soldiers had perished and Moscow had failed to take a major Ukrainian city. In the areas that Russia had managed to occupy, including traditionally Russian-speaking Kherson and Melitopol, Ukrainians took to the streets with blue-and-yellow flags. Kharkiv, the city on the Russian border where pro-Russian separatists had demonstrated in 2014, fought tooth and nail to defend itself against the aggressor.

On day two of the Ukrainian war, Vladimir Putin addressed the Ukrainian armed forces directly in a television broadcast. The Russian President looked pale and his tone was bleak. 'Do not allow neo-Nazis to use your children, women and elderly as human shields,' he said. 'Take matters into your own hands. I believe that we can come to an agreement with you more easily than with that mob of junkies and neo-Nazis that has taken control in Kyiv, and who are holding the entire Ukrainian people hostage.'

Exactly why Putin thought that anyone in the Ukrainian military would listen to what he had to say is a question for future historians of the greatest war in Europe since 1945.

What *is* certain is the fact that Putin underestimated both Zelensky and the entire Ukrainian people. On the night when Putin addressed the Ukrainian army, Zelensky recorded a brief video message in the heart of Kyiv. The Ukrainian President was dressed in military green, surrounded by members of his Cabinet. 'Good evening everybody,' said Zelensky. 'The President is here. Our armed forces are here, along with our whole society. We will defend our independence, our nation. Long live Ukraine!'

1. Al Pacino

Mariana and Yana, aged 17 and 18, have already managed to catch a glimpse of their heroes at a bar in the heart of Kharkiv. After loitering for some time outside the changing rooms to no avail, they finally decide just to sit down in the auditorium. Front-row centre, the best seats in the house.

The date is 10th September 2002, and Ukraine – like so many other countries – is in the midst of the internet explosion. By the end of the year, around 2.5 million of the country's 48 million inhabitants will be online. Mariana Belei is an early adopter, and writes gushing reviews of performances by her favourite team of comedians, who are led by a young Jewish man from the provincial town of Kryvyi Rih. Mariana is not alone in her pursuit: teenage girls all throughout Ukraine and Russia are writing page after page, blog after blog, on Volodymyr Zelensky.

Mariana and her friend wait in anticipation for a full 40 minutes. Finally the music starts, followed by eager applause. Afterwards she writes: 'Everybody's favourite, "Vova" Zelensky appeared on stage, and the show could begin.'

By that time, Mariana already knows the show inside out. Kvartal 95 has performed it in her home town three times. They deploy well-known sketches, such as the 'Spanish dance,' 'the manipulative therapist' and 'the actor.' The skits are highly physical, slapstick routines, and the actors tumble across the stage in black t-shirts and black leather pants.

The radiant linchpin and leader of the group is a lean young man with pitch-black hair, chiselled face, and a husky bass voice that is incongruous with his slight build. At first glance, Volodymyr Zelensky bears a likeness to the young Al Pacino, and his facial expressions occasionally resemble those of Rowan Atkinson, the comedian behind *Mr Bean*.

Kvartal 95's humour is well-tailored to public sensibilities. Ten years after the dissolution of the Soviet Union, the values of the utopian socialist state had crumbled, but the new liberal society was still in its infancy. While the whole country was happily firing heated criticism at its administration, sex was still taboo as a topic. Any such allusions made by Zelensky always brought the room to its knees.

'We laughed, laughed, and laughed again,' wrote Mariana in her online review. 'But then the final song came... the room erupted into thunderous applause.'

The 24-year-old young man on stage, Volodymyr Oleksandrovych Zelensky, comes from a line of assimilated Jews. When Nazi Germany invaded the Soviet Union in 1941, his grandfather Semyon Zelensky left for the front with his three brothers. Of the four, only Captain Semyon returned – wounded – to Kryvyi Rih. Semyon's parents had died when the Nazis burned their village to the ground.

After winning the presidential election, Zelensky was frequently asked about his Jewish heritage. He politely brushed the questions aside. 'We were a completely ordinary Soviet-Jewish family,' he said in an interview with the *Times of Israel* in 2020. 'Most Jewish families in the Soviet Union were not religious.'

Zelensky's parents were typical representatives of the Soviet intelligentsia. Zelensky's father, Oleksander, was a mathematician, and his mother Rymma worked as an engineer until she retired due to health reasons.

The family had one son: Volodymyr. In the early 1980s, the Zelenskys moved to Mongolia, where Oleksander took charge of a mining company. Rymma could not adapt to the harsh climate, with its scorching summers and ice-cold winters, and after four years returned to Kryvyi Rih with Volodymyr, leaving her husband behind. 'My father worked in Mongolia for nearly 20 years,' Zelensky later said. 'He gave Mongolia everything: his health, intellect, and the most important thing: time. Time he could have spent with me.'

Rymma and Volodymyr moved into a modest Soviet flat in the centre of Kryvyi Rih. Black-and-white photos from that period reveal an adorable little boy, with dark eyes and long black eyelashes. In one such photo, Rymma holds him up proudly on one arm. It is clear that the apple did not fall far from the tree.

Volodymyr was raised by his mother and grandmother. 'My mother still calls me every day,' Zelensky once said. And Vova always picks up. If he doesn't, Rymma will simply give him another call – or 10.

Zelensky's industrial home town does not have a rich cultural history. Kryvyi Rih literally means 'crooked horn' and refers to the sharp turn made by the Inhulets river as it meanders through the steppe before feeding into the mighty Dnipro. The first known written reference to Kryvyi Rih is in a document from 1739, which described it as a cluster of villages and winter camps belonging to the Cossacks, who then ruled the steppes. In the late-18th Century, the Russian Empire colonised southern Ukraine and the Black Sea region. After the sixth Russo-Turkish war (1768-1774), the Russian authorities funded an outpost in Kryvyi Rih. By the mid-19th Century it had grown into a military settlement, but was still far from a flourishing city.

The discovery of large iron-ore deposits changed all that, and transformed the Crooked Horn into the Kryvbas – one of the Soviet Union's largest industrial regions along with the

Donbas in eastern Ukraine and the Kuzbas in Siberia. Mines and smelting furnaces were built along the vast underground iron veins, and were soon accompanied by workers' homes. Modern-day Kryvyi Rih stretches out for nearly 50km, with endless ribbon development filling the gaps between the smokestacks and mineshafts.

Volodymyr Zelensky remembers the Kryvyi Rih of his youth as a sombre place. The large-scale extraction of iron ore from open mines filled the air with a red dust that clung to the lips and clogged the throat. Whenever it rained, the puddles on the asphalt turned blood-red. The fall of the Soviet Union and the end of the planned economy ushered in the demise of heavy industry, giving free reign to the black market, and rampant violence.

Iron ore was not the only thing that left red stains on the asphalt. From the late 80s, Kryvyi Rih was ravaged by youth gangs, known locally as 'runners.' The runners were regionally organised around streets and districts (*kvartaly*) and bore odd names such as 'the Bulls,' 'the Horses,' 'the Ninth,' 'For Nothing,' and even 'the Cabbage Rolls' – a favourite dish of Ukraine and Russia. The gangs 'raided' the territories of rival gangs, got into brawls, shot at one another using home-made guns, and extorted money from their peers in exchange for 'protection.' This was not organised crime as such. The fights were really a form of exaggerated hooliganism, and introduced some action into the youths' otherwise poor and mind-numbing existence. But they could be fatal. In an investigative piece on the runners in 2020, journalist Samuil Proskuryakov drew a comparison with the senseless violence in Anthony Burgess's *A Clockwork Orange*. In the roughly 10-year period that the runners ruled Kryvyi Rih, 28 teenagers and one police officer lost their lives. The youngest victim was 13 years old.

In the early 90s, Kryvyi Rih was not only a leader in youth crime: local mafia bosses had built up such a strong position that the city became known as the 'Ukrainian Palermo.' The Communist state-run businesses were managed either by shrewd young men who had gambled by taking out big loans, or by bandits who had eliminated the competition through intimidation and violence. Sometimes the line between entrepreneurs and mafia bosses in Kryvyi Rih was blurred: even 'honest' businesspeople surrounded themselves with thugs carrying AK-47s.

Luckily for an only child without a father, Volodymyr Zelensky lived in one of the greener central neighbourhoods, Kvartal 95, which was home to the intelligentsia and where the air was cleaner than in the outer suburbs.

The young Volodymyr was a bright pupil. But his first appearance in the school choir was no great success, as his music teacher Tetyana Solovyeva recalled years later: 'Even as a young child, he already had a deep bass. I swear to you, he spoke in a bass voice. I said fine, come and rehearse with us. I already knew what would happen. The children started singing, and he just grumbled a low "Ooooh, ooh ooh," everybody burst out laughing. And he even had the nerve to ask: "What are you all laughing at?"'

The mercurial Vova was at his best when he could move his body, such as during the wrestling lessons that his mother made him take as a form of self-defence, or the ballet lessons that he enthusiastically took. As a teenager, Vova Zelensky wore a ring in his ear, which in a town like Kryvyi Rih quickly raised suspicions of homosexuality, and was an open invitation to the city's thugs. To avoid violence, it was best to have a girl on one's arm.

Volodymyr attended Grammar School No. 95, one of the city's best schools. He listened to Beatles albums that the Soviet record company Melodia was permitted to release from the late 80s onwards, the perestroika era. The creative teenager wrote poetry and songs and played the guitar.

He was an enormous fan of soviet bard Vladimir Vysotsky (1938-1980). Volodymyr (the Ukrainian variant of 'Vladimir') not only shared the singer's namesake, but also his birthday, 25th January.

Zelensky's favourite Vysotsky song was one of the most famous, the theme song from the well-known 1967 film *Vertikal. Song About a Friend* tells of the camaraderie between mountain climbers: on the steep slopes of the Caucasus, where alpinists are dependent on each other for survival, the wheat is separated from the chaff, and you find out who your true friends are.

The young Zelensky was already interested in politics, and at the age of 16 dreamed of becoming a diplomat. If he had

had the chance, he would have chosen to study at the famous Moscow MGIMO academy for diplomats, the alma mater of the current Russian Minister for Foreign Affairs, Sergey Lavrov, and the spokesperson for his department, Maria Zakharova. Admission to the MGIMO was contingent on bribes, however, and the amounts were beyond anything that the young Zelensky could afford.

Young men in their late teens who do not go to university had to enter military service. But Zelensky did not see himself as a soldier, so he enrolled in a law degree in Kryvyi Rih. His father, Oleksander, thought that Volodymyr could have become a famous lawyer. Zelensky himself was less enthusiastic. 'I really wanted to go and study in Moscow,' he said later in an interview. 'When I had just started university [in Kryvyi Rih] I wanted to change degrees. But during my first year I ended up with KVN, and after that I didn't want to go anywhere else.'

The 1990s were the heyday of the international comedy talent shows that kept audiences throughout the Soviet Union glued to their televisions. While the history of KVN – the 'Club for the Joyful and Inventive' (*Klub Vesyolykh i Nakhodchivykh* in Russian) – goes back to the early 60s, the phenomenon did not gain real traction until the dissolution of the Soviet Union, when the show was run by a Russian host, Alexander Maslyakov.

Although the successor to the Soviet Union, the Commonwealth of Independent States proved dead in the water, the former members of the Soviet Republic still retained a strong communal culture, strengthened by their common use of the Russian language. KVN teams mushroomed in Kazakhstan, Georgia, and especially Russia, Ukraine, Belarus and Armenia. Amid the chaos and economic misery of the 1990s, the exuberant comedy contests were a weekly highlight – if you managed to catch them, that is.

In Armenia in the early 90s, for instance, power was scarce and TV broadcast for fewer than three hours a day. 'But every self-respecting Armenian had (and still has) their collection of VHS tapes with the recorded episodes of KVN shows,' wrote Anna Grigorian in the online edition of *Planet of the Diaspora*. At Armenian schools and universities, new KVN teams were constantly forming among groups of ambitious teenagers who dreamt of making it as comedy performers. Because of the sheer volume of willing participants, the KVN competitions were organised like football divisions. The premier league was, of course, held in Moscow.

The KVN sketches bear little resemblance to traditional Anglo-Saxon stand-up comedy. The scenes are presented by groups of actors organised into teams, with song and dance included as key elements. It is not uncommon for the punchline to be absent, with the joke residing in a gesture or a facial expression.

In the routine titled *Born to Dance*, for example, Zelensky played a man with a nervous tic. He cannot stop dancing, not even while being 'interviewed' about his condition on stage by a fellow team member, Denys Lushchyshyn. Zelensky's moves are so infectious that the interviewer involuntarily joins in, moving along with him. The two men dance across the stage cheek-to-cheek, with the audience in stitches.

'What nationality are you, by the way?' Lushchyshyn asks.

'I'm Russian,' Zelensky replies, 'and yourself?'

Taken aback, Lushchyshyn answers: 'Let's say I'm from Ukraine.'

Zelensky points his behind to Lushchyshyn, and the two men dance pressed up closely against one another, quasi doggy-style.

'Honestly though, Ukraine has always shafted Russia,' Zelensky calls out.

'Ugh, tell me about it,' says Lushchyshyn, 'You've got no clue what they're up to. First Ukraine sticks it to Russia...'

The two men swap places.

'... and then Russia screws Ukraine!'

The roots of Zelensky's KVN-team, Kvartal 95, lay in his immediate circle of friends, the young students that he sometimes hung around with at the fountain in Bohdan Khmelnytsky park. Many dreamed of appearing in the KVN shows on TV, but it was Zelensky who got scouted by one of the premier league teams of the day: Zaporizhzhia-Kryvyi Rih-Transit. The team members were all in their thirties, and in search of new blood. Zelensky had his television debut at age 18.

Two older members of Transit, Borys and Serhiy Shefir, would become Zelensky's friends for life. For a long time the trio not only shared an office together, but they were also neighbours, living just outside Kyiv.

Olena Kiyashko, an attractive, short-haired blonde, had known Zelensky from high school. One day they meet on the street. Olena was carrying a VHS tape of the film *Basic Instinct* in her hands. 'Oh, I've always wanted to see that!' Zelensky cried. 'Could I borrow it from you?' It was a barefaced lie – Zelensky, a confirmed film buff, had already seen Paul Verhoeven's erotic thriller at least 15 times. But the ploy gave him a reason to ask for Olena's telephone number – how else was he supposed to return the tape to her?

Olena knew who Zelensky was. Vova and his friends were local personalities, who livened up school events and other festivities with their performances. 'I didn't think we would start dating,' Olena later recalled. 'Those boys were always surrounded by the prettiest girls.' Up until the moment when Zelensky declared his love for Olena, she never thought anything of it. Once they were an item, Olena broke it off. 'I had romantic feelings for somebody else.' That was when Zelensky called her up for 'a very serious talk.'

'I told him that I had other plans for my life, and that we had to go our separate ways. But then he said a few things that got me thinking, about what I would be missing out on.'

Olena chose Vova. 'Once he's set his mind on something, he never lets go,' she said 16 years later, after 10 years of marriage.

When Transit began to dissolve in 1997, Zelensky got a new crew together. Other KVN teams always carefully constructed their teams from cookie-cutter personalities: a lead singer, a dancer, a comic talent, and sketch writers. To Zelensky,

Life partners: *Volodymyr Zelensky and Olena Zelenska.*
Ukraine Government

however, the most important factor was loyalty. Although Kvartal 95 would start out as a group of friends, it would grow into the most famous Ukrainian comedy team in history.

None of the members of Kvartal 95 had any training in the entertainment industry. Olena Kravets (b. 1977), the only woman in the troupe, studied financial economics. Oleksander Pikalov (b. 1976) earned his living as a street cleaner before beginning an engineering degree. Yuriy Krapov (b. 1973) worked as an electrical engineer in the mining industry. At the behest of his father, who wanted him to become a surgeon, Yuriy Koryavchenkov (b. 1974) worked for two years as a nurse in a local hospital.

In 1998, Kvartal 95 entered a competition in Sochi, the Russian spa town on the Black Sea. Reports say that KVN founder Maslyakov was especially impressed by the young law student Zelensky, and Kvartal 95 was invited to the grand final in Moscow. At that time, Kvartal 95 began touring through Ukraine and Russia. Its schedule was unrelenting, travelling over the pockmarked Ukrainian roads during the day (often by bus), and performing at night. Precious free time was taken up with writing new material and rehearsing new routines.

In 2001, Zelensky gave an interview to the local Siberian edition of *Moskovskiy Komsomolets*, the popular Moscow-based daily tabloid, after completing a tour of Siberia with Kvartal 95. He said that he enjoyed the icy winter weather: 'Back home the winters are grey, without snow.' The young comedian, the interviewer noted, spoke Russian with a 'cute accent.'

The 600,000 inhabitants of Kryvyi Rih are overwhelmingly Ukrainian, with ethnic Russians a minority (even the 15,000-strong Jewish community is larger). And yet for many, Russian is their native language. 'We grew up in families where nationalism was not very important,' said Zelensky in his interview with *Moskovskiy Komsomolets*. 'We speak Russian. The fact that others speak Ukrainian is no issue.' Even in the icy chill of the Kuzbas, thousands of kilometres from Kryvyi Rih, the young Zelensky felt as though he was living in 'one country.'

By then, Zelensky and his co-performers were already spending most of their time in Moscow, still the economic centre and cultural centre of the former Soviet Union. The young comedian's favourite places in Moscow were the famous theatre academies. 'My favourite actors walked these halls,' he said in an interview in 2008. 'I wanted to sit in the same lecture theatres, study the same roles as they did.' But again, money was a problem, so Zelensky opted for on-the-job training. 'I decided that if I couldn't take the traditional route through a theatre academy, I would complete the School of KVN. The road might be a longer one, but would be no less effective.'

Zelensky would not retain any fond memories of Moscow. 'Knock on someone's door in Moscow, and they don't open it. Not even your own neighbours.' The sophisticated Moscovites looked down on provincial types, who swarmed to the capital during the 90s.

Though the members of Kvartal 95 lived in Moscow, they had no fixed address. Registering with the local municipal council was impossible, so Zelensky and his comrades were always moving between hotels and apartments. Money was an ever-present problem. 'We were probably the poorest team in the history of KVN,' Zelensky recalled in 2008.

When on tour, the group always took their own food with them: bacon and potatoes. The actors shopped at the VDNKh All-Russia Exhibition Centre, the only place in Moscow that sold instant noodles. Zelensky said of their cooking: 'We prepared meals on an electric hotplate in our hotel room. The fire alarm often went off when we were trying to bake potatoes.'

Not that nobody earned anything from the immensely popular KVN. The host and manager, Alexander Maslyakov, was the copyright owner and the sole shareholder of the production company that made the shows. TV stations from across the Soviet Union paid top dollar for the broadcasting rights, and because of the enormous viewership, sponsors were eager to advertise. Maslyakov was only too happy to oblige, and would gladly drop the name of a particular brand several times over the course of a show. All the revenue went to Maslyakov and the competitors received nothing – not even reimbursement of their travel or accommodation expenses. The Russian media would speak of the 'Maslyakov pyramid scheme,' while the participants referred to the producer as 'His Majesty.' Those who did not fall in line were excluded from the competition.

Whenever Kvartal 95 organised performances under the banner of KVN, they were forced to surrender a portion of the takings to Maslyakov – some Russian media sources placed the amount at up to 40 per cent. A gig in the provinces paid no more than US$600, which had to be shared among the whole team.

'We hardly have enough to live on,' Zelensky recounted in 2001. 'I have no car, no house, I live on what I get from our shows. It's hardly enough to keep the wolves at bay.'

Because Kvartal 95 was under such constant financial strain, the team was unable to purchase ready-made routines, in the way that some other teams could. They wrote all of their sketches themselves. Zelensky worked late into the night after performances, or on the bus during the day on the way to the next show. In an interview in 2002, he said that when writing new material, he got so engrossed that he forgot to shave. On the streets of Moscow, the police would stop him and ask to see his papers, to make sure he was not a Chechen terrorist.

Asked about his free time, Zelensky said: 'I've forgotten what that is! I like to return home now and again, to Kryvyi Rih, to visit my parents. I get relaxation from everything I enjoy. Like winning a competition.'

The only hobby Zelensky permitted himself was watching movies – with the aim of improving his technique. According to an interview in 2001, he had a clear goal in mind, though he refused to say exactly what that was.

Although Kvartal 95 was one of the top KVN teams, it missed out on the finals on several occasions. 'I hate talking about failures,' said Zelensky in 2002, after the team lost in the semi-finals. 'If we are to win, we need to be 10 times better than the teams from St. Petersburg or Moscow. We're just the lads from Kryvyi Rih.'

However, 'the lads from Kryvyi Rih' had amassed quite a female following. Wherever they went, the members of Kvartal 95 were mobbed by hordes of screaming girls. And although most of the attention was directed at the group's leader, Zelensky seemed largely unaffected.

On Valentine's Day, one of the Ukrainian television stations ran a contest for viewers. Whoever wrote the most romantic love letter would win a dinner for two with their idol.

Kateryna Derba, aged 27, wrote to Zelensky:

First you came to live in my thoughts, then in my heart. I did my utmost to push you out, but you refused to leave. I became angry... what is wrong with me? How can such a thing happen to a grown woman?

Kateryna feverishly went in search of more information on her hero. Following her sister's advice, she trawled the official KVN website – all 53 pages – for insights. 'I learned that people love and respect you, and that they are – unsurprisingly – jealous. Compared to other people, your career stands out a mile.'

Kateryna Derba was right: Zelensky's star was rising. And with foresight, she described his future in her letter: 'I believe that we will soon see you on our TV screens, saying: "Dear Citizens of Ukraine!"'

2. Bad Neighbours

Time: the year 2000, during the second semi-final of the Ukrainian KVN championships.

Place: the October Palace in Kyiv.

Competitors: Kvartal 95, team Loud! from Kyiv, and 4 Tatarina from Kazan, Russia.

The event: improvisation – one team provides the setup, the other must shoot for the goal.

Volodymyr Zelensky, then aged 22, kicks off: 'Sir Leonid Kuchma challenges Sir Vladimir Putin to a duel!'

Quiet sniggers are heard throughout the auditorium.

(By way of background, Leonid Kuchma has been re-elected in 1999 as the second President of Ukraine. And after Boris Yeltsin unexpectedly resigns on 31st December 1999, Vladimir Putin has become President of the Russian Federation.)

Team Loud! try to bring home the laughs, but their efforts fall short.

'Would you care to take a shot yourselves?' host Alexander Maslyakov asks Kvartal 95.

Zelensky steps up to the microphone. 'Sir Leonid Kuchma challenges Sir Vladimir Putin to a duel. One knight says to the other: "My good sir, here in Russia, we have gas. And what do you have?" "We," says the other fellow, "have the pipeline!"'

The room erupts in laughter. Under Putin, Russia was experiencing an economic boom, due principally to the export of oil and gas. But in order to sell these resources, they first needed to be transported through Ukrainian territory, via Ukrainian pipelines. For every cubic metre of Russian gas that was sent to Germany, Ukraine imposed a transport surcharge. So while oil prices (and with them, the price of gas) rose to record heights in the late 90s, Ukraine's centralised heating remained dirt-cheap.

In 1991, the Soviet Union fell apart, and Ukraine gained independence. For those in the Kremlin, it was a bitter reality. Within months, military tensions were rising between the two countries. In 1954, the Soviet leader, Nikita Khrushchev, had transferred the Crimean Peninsula from the Russian to the Ukrainian Socialist Soviet Republic. Though inconsequential at the time, this administrative reshuffle became a major faultline after the dissolution of the Soviet Union in 1991.

From one day to the next, Crimea – with its predominantly ethnic-Russian population – had become part of Ukraine. According to the new government in Kyiv, this meant that the strategic Black Sea Fleet also had become Ukrainian. But Moscow was not about to give up its navy without a battle, and in the spring of 1992, irregularities emerged at the port in Sevastopol. Some ships' crews flew the Ensign of the Russian Navy, or St. Andrew's flag – a diagonal blue cross on a white background – while other ships hoisted the blue-and-yellow of Ukraine.

In April 1992, Russian Vice-President Alexander Rutskoy flew to Sevastopol. During a speech given to the officers of the fleet, Rutskoy not only declared that the navy in the harbour was Russian, but maintained that Khrushchev must have been hungover (or perhaps he had sunstroke) when he reapportioned Crimea to Ukraine. Whatever the case: 'The Crimean Peninsula undoubtedly belonged to Russia.'

It was a serious threat. The next day, the Ukrainian President, Leonid Kravchuk, issued an ukase (a kind of presidential decree or executive order) placing the Black Sea Fleet under Ukrainian command. Two days later, the Russian President Yeltsin signed his own ukase, placing the fleet 'under the jurisdiction of the Russian Federation.' For a short time, the 'ukase war' threatened to escalate into a military confrontation.

Until, that is, Kravchuk called Yeltsin and the Presidents arrived at a compromise. Slowly over five years, the ships of the Black Sea Fleet would be redistributed. Russia was also granted the provisional right to use the harbour at Sevastopol. 'Yeltsin was an imperialist, but he was well aware of what he could and could not do,' Kravchuk said during an interview in 2016. 'He could be reasoned with. If we'd had a similar situation with Putin, he would have opened fire straight away.'

Even though Boris Yeltsin deliberately brought about the end of the Soviet Union, many in Moscow saw the loss of territory as a humiliating defeat, and nothing was more painful than the forced farewell to Ukraine.

In the mid-1990s, an American analyst, Zbigniew Brzeziński, captured the relationship between the two countries. 'Without Ukraine, Russia ceases to be an empire,' Jimmy Carter's former security adviser said.

If you view history through a Russian lens, an unbroken line runs from the Kyivan Empire (882-1240) through to the Russian Empire (1721-1917) to the Soviet Union (1922-1991) and the current Russian Federation. This Russia-centric view of history does not grant Ukraine the status of an independent nation, with its own language and culture. While it is often said in Moscow that Russians and Ukrainians are 'brothers,' Ukraine is always the 'little' brother.

There is no dispute that both nations share the same roots. The Kyivan Empire, Kyivan Rus' (*Kiyevskaya Rus'* in Russian), came into being on the river Dnipro. According to the most accepted theories, Scandinavian traders and warriors known as the Varangians (Vikings), or Rus', established settlements as they travelled along the river from the Baltic Sea to the Black Sea, the gateway to the Byzantine Empire. The Primary Chronicle, the first manuscript documenting the history of Rus' around 1113, refers to the Varangian Rurik as the ancestral father of a dynasty of Kyivan rulers. Rurik's successor, Oleg the Wise, (879-912) conquered Kyiv, a fortified settlement on the right bank of the Dnipro. Other important administrative centres emerged, such as Veliki Novgorod, Rostov Veliki, and Vladimir – all cities that now lie in Russia.

Oleg's grandson, Vladimir the Great (or Saint Vladimir or Volodymyr in Ukrainian 978-1015) converted to Christianity. Both Zelensky and Putin share his namesake.

The Russian history books present the Kyivan rulers as the first Russian 'tsars.' But Rurik and his successors were actually Vikings from modern-day Sweden and spoke Old Norse. The subjugated population spoke Old East Slavic, the ancestor of the modern Eastern Slavic languages of Belarusian, Ukrainian and Russian.

By the mid-12th Century, the Kyivan Empire had cleaved into three principalities: the Novgorod Republic and Vladimir-Suzdal in the north and the kingdom of Galicia–Volhynia in the west. From 1237 onwards, the Mongolians started conquering the East Slavic principalities, and it was not until the 15th Century that Moscow (whose name does not appear in manuscripts until the mid-12th Century) extricated itself from Mongolian rule. Other parts of Rus' were conquered by the kingdom of Lithuania and were governed from the 16th Century by the Polish-Lithuanian Commonwealth, or *Rzeczpospolita*.

For a little over two centuries, what we now know as Ukraine was divided into separate territories. The Dnipro formed the eastern border of the Polish-Lithuanian Commonwealth: Kyiv was a 'Polish' city. On the opposite bank, the Moscovian Empire gained ground. Beyond the rapids to the south, the Cossacks ruled the steppes and tried to distance themselves from both centres of power.

Not until the late-18th Century would the Russian Empire take the coast of the Black Sea and share the weakened Polish state with Prussia and Austria. From 1772-1795, the lion's share of modern-day Ukraine became Russian territory, with the exception of West Galicia, which was held by Austria.

In the imperial capital of St. Petersburg, the name 'Ukraine' was never actually used. The left and right banks of the Dnipro were collectively referred to as 'Little Russia' (*Malorossia*), and the conquered Ottoman region on the Black Sea as 'New Russia' (*Novorossia*). St. Petersburg saw Ukrainians as a kind of apostate Russians, and the Ukrainian language as a Russian dialect.

The language was systematically suppressed. From the reign of Peter the Great (1672-1725), books that had previously appeared in Ukrainian were henceforth published only in Russian. In 1794, Russian became the compulsory language at the famous academy in Kyiv, then one of the most eminent theological centres of the Eastern Orthodox world.

In the early-19th Century, under the influence of the Romantic period, intellectuals in Little Russia began to rediscover their own language and culture, and the term 'Ukraine' was born. Shortly after the great Russian poet Alexander Pushkin (1799-1837) had almost single-handedly created literary Russian, the liberated serf Taras Shevchenko (1814-1861) wrote epic verses that would lay the foundations for Ukrainian literature. The Russian authorities saw this kind of 'Ukrainophilia' as a political threat and in the second half of the 19th Century, devised ways of suppressing Ukrainian literature.

In the 20th Century, the region experienced one catastrophe after another. After its revolution, Russia was ravaged by an all-encompassing civil war (1917-1922). In Ukraine, Bolsheviks (the 'Reds') fought against tsarist troops (the 'Whites'), and Ukrainian nationalists battled against Poles and Bolsheviks. In 1932 and 1933, Stalin's forced agricultural collectivisation policies gave rise to a horrific famine, the Holodomor. During World War II, Ukraine once again lay on the front lines. Between 1917 and 1945, around 15-20 million Ukrainians (including 900,000 Jews) died as the result of hunger, war and genocide.

Ukrainian attempts to found an independent state amid the chaos were short-lived. The People's Republic of Ukraine, declared in 1917, was trampled underfoot by the Red Army in 1920. During World War II, a radical nationalist, Stepan Bandera, tried to realise independence by collaborating with the Nazis. From 1944, Bandera's rebel army – the UPA – fought both German soldiers and the Red Army. Soviet propaganda portrayed Bandera (who was ultimately 'liquidated' by the

KGB in Munich in 1959) as a diabolical figure. To Ukrainian nationalists, he was a hero.

After World War II, the Ukrainian Soviet Socialist Republic became the granary of the Soviet Union, and a repository for heavy industry. Slowly but surely, the process of Russification continued. From 1954, speaking the Ukrainian language was no longer necessary for admission to higher education. In 1958, Russian became mandatory in all schools in the Soviet Republic, and Ukrainian became a subject of choice. The consequences were dramatic. In the 1970s, the proportion of Ukrainian journals fell from 46 to 19 percent, and the number of books published in Ukrainian fell from 49 to 24 percent.

In some ways, the Ukraine that was suddenly granted independence in late 1991 was an orphaned country. According to research by the National Academy of Sciences of Ukraine in Kyiv, in 1992 only 36.8 per cent of the population spoke Ukrainian at home. Russian was spoken almost exclusively in major cities such as Kharkiv, Donetsk, Odessa, and the capital Kyiv. While Ukrainian dominated the west, Russian was the principal language in the south and the east.

The People's Movement of Ukraine (*Narodnyi Rukh Ukrajiny*), launched in 1989, had its roots mainly in the Ukrainian-speaking west. But as the Soviet leader, Mikhail Gorbachev, slowly but surely loosened the reins, the notion of separation quickly gained momentum. In the spring of 1990, more-or-less democratic elections were held for the first time throughout the various Soviet Socialist Republics, giving the local 'soviets' (parliaments) an unprecedented voice. When the Russian Soviet Federative Socialist Republic adopted a Declaration of State Sovereignty, so too did the Ukrainian parliament, the *Verkhovna Rada*.

In an attempt to preserve the rapidly-disintegrating Soviet Union, Gorbachev organised a referendum in the spring of 1991 asking citizens whether they were in favour of a 'renewed federation of equal and sovereign republics.' The question was couched so vaguely that 70 per cent of the Ukrainian population voted in favour of the new Union. Only in the western provinces and Kyiv was there a majority against.

Not everybody in the West was eager for an independent Ukrainian state. On 1st August of that same year, the American President, George H.W. Bush, gave a speech before the Verkhovna Rada, expressing his support for Gorbachev's new Union. The agreement, Bush said, 'holds forth the hope that Republics will combine greater autonomy with greater voluntary interaction – political, social, cultural, economic – rather than pursuing the hopeless course of isolation.'

Within three weeks, Bush's 'Chicken Kiev' speech, as it became known, was obsolete. On 18th August 1991, Communist hardliners staged a coup in Moscow, but the Russian tanks were stopped by peaceful activists directed by Boris Yeltsin, President of Russia. The failed August coup spelled the end of Soviet Russia. Ukraine, too, looked on with horror at the events unfolding in Moscow. In an extraordinary session on 24th

August, the Ukrainian Parliament declared its independence, in anticipation of a new referendum. For the first time, the chamber was adorned with the blue-and-yellow Ukrainian flag. On 1st December, 90.3 per cent of voters (on a turnout of 84.2 per cent) voted for independence. Even in the Russian-speaking regions of Luhansk and Donetsk, more than 80 per cent voted in favour of Ukraine becoming an independent state.

On 8th December, at a hunting lodge on the border of Poland and Belarus, the leaders of Russia, Belarus and Ukraine signed an accord that dissolved the Soviet Union for good. In his memoirs, Boris Yeltsin recalls the almost solemn atmosphere that pervaded the room as the three Presidents placed their signatures: 'I still remember it well, there in the Białowieża Forest, the air was suddenly filled with a sense of freedom and lightness. Russia had chosen a peace-loving, democratic and non-imperial path for its future development.' The Ukrainian President, Leonid Kravchuk, saw the situation quite differently. He said later: 'Ukraine can be proud to have been the country that sent the Soviet Union to its grave.'

Kravchuk was a former party heavyweight, a Communist ideologue from west Ukraine who had worked his way up to Chairman of the Supreme Soviet. Still, he was no die-hard nationalist. Like their Russian counterparts, the Ukrainian apparatchiks primarily saw the end of the Soviet Union as an ideal opportunity to expand their own spheres of power and influence. Kravchuk made overtures to the West, but he was in no hurry to reform his state's bankrupt economy. To keep government businesses running, Kravchuk simply printed more money, causing hyperinflation. In 1993, Ukrainians headed to supermarkets carrying shopping bags full of banknotes. Meanwhile, the average income in the same year was still less than US$50 per month. In smaller, rural towns, a barter economy emerged.

Despite its financial difficulties, the bankrupt country was still the third largest nuclear power after Russia and the United States. Even after surrendering its tactical nuclear weapons to Russia, Kyiv still had 176 intercontinental rockets and 1,700 nuclear warheads – weapons whose use-by date would expire in 1998. Because Ukraine had neither the means nor the technology to maintain the arsenal, Kravchuk decided to divest himself of the weapons. In 1994, the Memorandum of Budapest was signed, in which Ukraine as well as Belarus and Kazakhstan relinquished their nuclear weaponry. In exchange, the United States, Great Britain and the Russian Federation agreed to safeguard the countries' sovereignty and territorial borders – a promise that Moscow would break 20 years later.

In 1993, the dire economic situation sparked protests throughout Ukraine, and President Kravchuk had no choice but to call an early presidential election, which he lost to his former premier, Leonid Kuchma. The first democratic transfer of power was effected, unlike in Belarus and Russia, where the budding democracies would crystallise into authoritarian regimes.

Under Kuchma, the economic situation in Ukraine stabilised, partly due to the introduction of a new national currency, the hryvnia. In 1996, a new constitution was enacted. The Russian Federation had opted for a presidential system that handed exorbitant powers to the head of state. Ukraine chose a semi-presidential model that gave a significant role to Parliament.

Kuchma's first order of business was to privatise the old state-run businesses, which massively concentrated wealth in the hands of a few rich individuals: oligarchs. In Donetsk, Rinat Akhmetov and his 'clan' took possession of the coal mines and the Donbas chemical industry. In Dnipro, Viktor Pinchuk took charge of the metal industry. Viktor Medvedchuk ruled in the capital of Kyiv.

To obtain tax benefits and influence over legislation, Ukraine's new oligarchs bribed judges and parliamentarians and tried to take control of the media. Within a few years, each clan controlled a TV station and political party. Political life in Ukraine had mutated into a battle for commercial interests.

The uncontested head of the new kleptocracy was Kuchma himself. His daughter, Olena, married the head of the Dnipro clan, Viktor Pinchuk, and rumours quickly spread that Pinchuk was not the only one calling the Ukrainian President 'papa.' The media started referring to the President as 'father of the oligarchs.'

As President, Kuchma manoeuvred shrewdly between Russia and the West. He appeased Moscow by signing a comprehensive friendship treaty and devoted extensive attention to the Commonwealth of Independent States, the successor to the Soviet Union, which Russia regarded as key to its ongoing influence. At the same time, he signed a cooperation agreement with NATO, and alluded to potential membership. In 1997, American marines conducted exercises in Crimea, near the Russian garrison in Sevastopol – much to the Kremlin's chagrin.

That same year, Kuchma and the Russian President Yeltsin signed an agreement on the future of Crimea. The Black Sea Fleet was divided between Ukraine and Russia. The peninsula itself would remain part of Ukraine, but Russia would retain the right to use the harbour in Sevastopol for another 10 years. The deal sparked furious debate in the Russian Parliament, and the agreement was not ratified by Moscow until 1999.

In 2000, a series of corruption scandals discredited Kuchma in the West. One of Kuchma's bodyguards had secretly recorded hundreds of hours' worth of the President's conversations, and made some of them public. The Kuchma tapes revealed that Ukraine's leader had no problem selling advanced radar systems to Iraqi dictator Saddam Hussein, as well as his order to 'have something done' about journalist and founder of *Ukrainska Pravda,* Georgiy Gongadze, whose decapitated and heavily mutilated body was discovered in November 2000. When the tapes were played in the Rada, the Ukrainian people heard how their leader screamed, swore, and spat out antisemitic abuse. Kuchma denied that it was his voice.

When his term ended in 2003, the Ukrainian President made a desperate – and unconstitutional – attempt to win a third term. When he failed, he focused on finding a successor who would maintain the status quo and indemnify him from criminal prosecution. Rinat Akhmetov's Donetsk clan supplied the suitable candidate: Viktor Yanukovych.

Yanukovych had a deep bass voice and no charisma. He was orphaned at an early age, had criminal charges for theft and abuse to his name, and most probably purchased all of his academic titles, given the spelling errors in the certificates. In all likelihood he had filled them out himself: one of them contained the word 'professor' spelled with two f's.

In that same year, 2003, Zelensky and the members of Kvartal 95 were still living and working in Moscow for KVN. However, relations with director Alexander Maslyakov had soured. Malsyakov and Zelensky fought over money and freedom of expression. In 2001, Putin had forced a media magnate, Vladimir Gusinsky, to give up his independent TV station, NTV. Other channels were also informed that criticism of the President would no longer be tolerated.

KVN, too, was subject to censorship. When a staff member of the production company deleted a large number of Zelensky's jokes from one episode, he marched straight up to Maslyakov. 'His Majesty' was not amused. 'We were told that KVN could manage easily without us,' team member Borys Shefir recalled. 'So we said that we were planning to leave anyway.' Several days later, Kvartal 95 – indisputably one of the best teams in the KVN world – was eliminated from the quarter finals. Zelensky was furious at Maslyakov: 'We worshipped this man, and he washed his hands of us.'

Still, Maslyakov was not ready to bid Zelensky a final farewell. According to one version of events, the director made Zelensky a proposal, offering him a well-paid position as one of the lead writers for the show – on condition that he leave behind his teammates from Kvartal 95. Zelensky refused.

Another version has Kvartal 95 leaving when Maslyakov wanted to withhold an even larger portion of the team's revenue. Whatever happened, Zelensky and friends returned to Kyiv. It was a bold move, but the timing was right. After almost 10 years of economic decline, Ukraine experienced growth for the first time in 2000. In 2003, GDP rose by a spectacular 9.5 per cent.

The growth was due not to Kuchma, but rather to Viktor Yushchenko, the charming President of the National Bank of Ukraine whom Kuchma had appointed Prime Minister in 1999. Yushchenko possessed a quality that was unique in the Ukrainian political landscape of the day: integrity. The new premier was an outspoken liberal, which was helpful in his negotiations with the International Monetary Fund (IMF), with whom Ukraine had amassed mountains of debt. Alongside Deputy Prime Minister Yulia Tymoshenko, Yushchenko started taking action against a shady billion-dollar business in the gas market. Around 80 per cent of the gas sold to Europe was transported through Ukrainian pipelines. Kyiv only paid a fraction of the world price for the gas and also charged transport levies to the supplier, Russia, which paid in kind with more gas. These transactions gave rise to a blossoming intermediary market rife with tax avoidance, the theft of Russian gas, and the illegal onsale of gas to Europe. Tymoshenko knew the business like no other, for she herself had earned a fortune this way.

Yushchenko and Tymoshenko also decided to trim the many tax benefits that the oligarchs had arranged for themselves with the help of their friends in the Government and Parliament. Yushchenko's reforms furnished the treasury with US$4 billion in 2000 alone – equivalent to 13 per cent of GDP. For the first time, the Ukrainian government could afford to pay pensions and government salaries, which sharply increased household spending. In Kyiv and other large cities, the first contours of a middle class began to emerge.

Zelensky and his team settled in Kyiv. But in a country where they had no connections and where corruption was the norm, they had difficulty finding work. 'It was a big adventure,' Serhiy Shefir recalled. 'The big media bosses in Kyiv told us: there are hundreds more in line before you. You won't get anywhere.'

Kvartal 95 lived from occasional gigs and scriptwriting jobs from Moscow, which the team carried out under various pseudonyms. 'We were all very worried about the future,' said actor Yuriy Krapov. But the friends were ecstatic with their new-found freedom. 'We were beholden to nobody,' Olena Kravets would later say in an interview. 'We didn't have to submit our scripts to anyone for approval, there was no censorship at all.'

At the time, Zelensky was living in a rundown hotel room on the outskirts of Kyiv, arranged for him by a studio director he knew.

In September 2003, Volodymyr Zelensky married Olena Kiyashko. The reception was held at a bowling club in Kryvyi Rih, the only affordable venue that could accommodate 100 guests. The groom stood beside his beaming bride in a hired suit that looked several sizes too big.

The next day, Zelensky left for Kyiv on business. That was the day when Zelensky and Borys and Serhiy Shefir – his partners from day one – founded their production company, Studio Kvartal 95. Zelensky drove to business meetings with the Shefir brothers in his old jalopy, a rundown Lada estate car. He never parked by the front door, always around the corner. 'I realised that I couldn't present myself to serious companies with such a disgraceful car,' Zelensky recalled in 2008. 'All the potential sponsors said the same thing: "We'll have a think, we need to discuss it." We could hardly press them, saying: "Don't think too long, we need to pay our rent."'

Zelensky and Olena settled permanently in Kyiv. They shared a one-bedroom apartment with the Shefir brothers, their mother, and a dog. Only after one year did the business partners earn enough to afford separate homes. In 2004, Zelensky's first child, Oleksandra (Sasha), was born. She was named after Zelensky's father, who was thrilled.

To make ends meet, Zelensky became presenter of a cooking show titled *Mr Cook*, despite the fact that he could barely manage an omelette. Although the job brought in more than the Shefir brothers' writing gigs, all the money went into a communal fund. The script writing may have been less lucrative, but everyone shared a common goal: to win over Ukraine. Though Zelensky and his comrades were working on their careers in Kyiv, a large portion of their income still came from Russia. That changed at the end of 2003, when Kvartal 95 put on a New Year's spectacular in Kyiv, and tickets sold like hot cakes. Producers from the TV station 1+1 were impressed, and offered the team a contract. Kvartal made five television programmes and gave additional theatre shows, performing around 10-15 times per month. The shows consisted of short sketches, supplemented with well-known Russian and Ukrainian pop acts. The jokes were innocent, revolved around relationships, day-to-day life and – occasionally – the impoverished state of the country.

'They say that if you wake up in the morning and nothing hurts, you're dead,' said Zelensky at the end of a show titled *The Matrix*.

He left an extra-long pause.

'Our economy is in a bad way, the entertainment industry is enough to make your skin crawl, and our football team is a shocking embarrassment. I guess that means we're all still alive!'

Kvartal 95 wanted to continue producing for 1+1, but despite Zelensky's lobbying efforts, the management saw no place for Volodymyr and his companions. Interest in comedy had waned in the summer of 2004, as the entire country was caught up in the presidential elections.

The race was between two Viktors – Viktor Yushchenko, the former central banker with integrity, and the rougher candidate from the Donetsk clan: Viktor Yanukovych. The battle between the two Viktors was a battle between east and west: between those wanting a pro-Western liberal Ukraine, and those determined to maintain the Moscow-backed status quo.

The pro-Russian Yanukovych rigged the election and won. But Ukrainians didn't take it lying down.

3. The Comedy Factory

On 26th October 2004, five days before the Ukrainian elections, Russian President Vladimir Putin flew to Kyiv. Although the pro-Russian candidate, Viktor Yanukovych, had run the 'most sordid election campaign in history' (according to the incumbent President, Leonid Kuchma), he was still behind in the polls.

For the state visit, Putin and Kuchma piggy-backed on an historical anniversary. On 28th October 1944, the Red Army chased the last of the German troops out of the Ukrainian Soviet Republic. The platinum celebrations were to be accompanied by a large military parade in the centre of Kyiv. To add more grandeur, Putin brought the red flag with him that the Soviet troops had hoisted above the Berlin Reichstag building in 1945.

No sooner had Putin arrived in the country than he gave an interview that was broadcast live simultaneously by three channels. It was an unprecedented event in Ukrainian television: the New Year's speech by President Kuchma had been the only previous event in the country's history to be broadcast live on multiple channels. A dedicated website called Ask Putin gave Ukrainians the opportunity to submit questions. The next day, the Russian papers would report that 80,000 Ukrainian citizens had done so. Viewers could also call in during the interview.

Putin was as forthcoming as possible.

'I am very fond of the Ukrainian language,' said the Russian President. 'I can still remember some words and phrases, in my student days I tried to read *The Bard*.' He then trotted out a few memorised verses of the famous work by Ukraine's national poet, Taras Shevchenko:

The days and nights, they come, forsooth;
And as my hands caress my brow,
I wonder: harbinger of truth,
O wisdom's witness, where art thou?

'Those are the only lines I can remember, probably because that's how I myself felt at the time,' Putin joked – referring to his years at the KGB Academy in Moscow. 'Unfortunately I don't speak any Ukrainian.'

Putin's interest in Ukraine did not come out of the blue. The Kremlin had already invested all its hopes in the man chosen by the incumbent President as his successor: Viktor Yanukovych. His opponent, Viktor Yushchenko, the honest former central banker, espoused liberal and pro-Western policies, and the Kremlin feared he might eventually drive Ukraine outside the sphere of Russian influence.

In the previous year, Putin's interest in his immediate neighbours had increased. Although rebels still resisted here and there, the Second Chechen War seemed more or less resolved. But now Putin had other problems. In 2003, the Georgians had ousted their President, Eduard Shevardnadze, who had been Gorbachev's Foreign Affairs Minister in the USSR. The 'Rose Revolution' was of concern to the Kremlin, as the new President, Mikheil Saakashvili, had studied law at Columbia University, spoke fluent English, and was pushing for both EU and NATO membership for Georgia.

The same fate for Ukraine was to be avoided at all costs, and so the Kremlin sent its best spin doctors to Kyiv to aid Yanukovych. At Putin's behest, Russian oligarchs reputedly ploughed US$300 million into the election campaign for the ex-prime minister, who came from the Russian-speaking Donbas region. Yanukovych and his advisers pulled out the traditional Russian playbook. The TV stations controlled by President Kuchma and his fellow oligarchs denied Yushchenko any air time, and his campaign was constantly disrupted by strange incidents. A local airport refused landing to Yushchenko's aircraft not once but twice, necessitating detours via other airports. The government-controlled media branded Yushchenko, whose roots were in western Ukraine, as a nationalist, Bandera-acolyte and a Nazi. Voters received leaflets in the mail claiming that the opposition candidate had had his first wife murdered, despite the fact that she was alive and well.

On 5th September, Yushchenko dined with the leaders of the SBU, the Ukrainian secret service. When he became unwell, he was rushed to Vienna for urgent medical treatment. Medical investigation later revealed that he had suffered dioxin poisoning. The presidential candidate recovered, but his face was scarred permanently by the acne caused by the toxin.

The first election on 31st October was inconclusive. At the second election, held on 21st November, Yanukovych obtained 49.5 per cent of the vote, and Yushchenko 46.6 per cent.

It became apparent that there had been large-scale election fraud, and hundreds of thousands of voters gathered on Maidan Nezalezhnosti (Independence Square) in Kyiv. The demonstrators waved orange flags, the colour adopted by the Yushchenko-Tymoshenko coalition. Despite the icy winter weather, the protests continued for weeks. The demonstrators camped out on the square in tents, and volunteers handed out hot soup. The threat of revolution was hanging in the air.

When observers from the Organization for Security and Co-operation in Europe confirmed that the elections were the fraudulent, the tide turned in favour of Yushchenko. The Ukrainian Supreme Court nullified the previous election result, and at the third election on 26th December, Yushchenko won with 52 per cent of the vote against Yanukovych's 44 per cent.

The 'Orange Revolution' in Kyiv was not only a scandal for Putin, it shook his regime. To nip potential future revolutions in the bud, the Kremlin launched its own militant youth movement: Nashi ('Our People'). If ever protests were to break out on the Red Square, the Kremlin would have a gang of citizenry to send out onto the streets, or at least that was the idea. To keep neighbouring countries within the Russian sphere of influence, a special secret-service department was created: the Department of Operational Information. Its officers were sighted in Belarus, Moldova and Abkhazia, particularly around election time. An FSB officer, Sergey Beseda, became head of the new department, and would resurface at pivotal moments.

In 2014, the protests put Ukraine on the world stage. Foreign TV crews eagerly filmed the hundreds of thousands of protesters in the biting cold on Maidan Square. But the 'revolution' would not bring about any significant reforms. Yushchenko's victory, furthermore, could not hide the fact that a clear divide was opening up in Ukraine. The predominantly Ukrainian-speaking central and western regions voted en masse for the opposition and a pro-western future. The Russian-speaking Crimea and the eastern provinces supported Yanukovych and his ties to Moscow.

Zelensky's parents, too, voted for Yanukovych and his Party of Regions. Zelensky's fellow performer and childhood friend, Oleksander Pikalov, did the same, which led to political discussions within Kvartal, as Zelensky later recalled: '"Don't get so worked up about it, Sasha," I often said. "Vova," he would reply, "that is our region, we come from the east!" "Sasha," I answered, "we come from the same country, we are from all regions. You're welcome everywhere: in Donetsk, where we've had awesome shows, and in Lviv." But he still argued back. He is radical by nature.'

In Kvartal 95's new show, Zelensky played President Yushchenko and Oleksander Pikalov played Yanukovych. Pikalov presented the leader of the Party of Regions as a criminal from the streets, and a not-too-bright one at that.

After their first successful TV shows, 1+1 strung Zelensky along for some time about the prospect of a sequel. Studio Kvartal 95 therefore switched to Inter, one of the country's largest TV stations. The management was prepared to take the plunge with a new programme titled *Vecherniy Kvartal* ('Kvartal by Night'). Zelensky envisaged a theatre-style show, with stand-up comedy interspersed with skits and appearances by popular artists. Kvartal member Valeriy Zhidkov later recalled that the Inter management imposed one condition: 'Jokes about politics were absolutely mandatory.'

Even in the very first episode of *Vecherniy Kvartal*, Zelensky played President Yushchenko. Beaming with pride, the newly-elected President walked on stage wheeling a rickety old 'Ukraine,' a Soviet brand of bicycle from Kharkiv.

'Look,' he said, 'I've scored myself a real Ukraine.'

In the audience, the penny dropped immediately. 'Disgraceful!' heckled a woman from the auditorium, but Zelensky retained his composure.

'The owner refused to part with it at first,' he continued. 'I had to ask three times before he said yes.'

TV star: *Volodymyr Zelensky recording a Kvartal 95 show in May 2018.* IMAGO/Pacific Press Agency

Zelensky imitated Yushchenko's solemn diction, and also gave the impression that the new President was a weakling, under the thumb of his political partner, Yulia Tymoshenko.

'I shall have a second saddle fitted for my girlfriend,' said the President with a blissful smile. 'I will do the pedalling, while she steers.'

The President then switched from Russian to Ukrainian: 'Druzi! ('Friends!') I will take all of you to Europe on this bicycle. It is the only one we have.'

The audience clapped themselves silly, and the next day's performance was completely sold out. It dawned on Zelensky that he had found a formula for success.

The Orange Revolution was a magical awakening for Ukraine, and the country's politics provided a rich source of spectacle. President Yushchenko and his coalition partner Tymoshenko took their bickering to the streets, and the great coalition degenerated into conflict – to their rival Yanukovych's advantage. In public, the lanky oaf from Donbas cut a poor figure, but proved himself a sly politician behind the scenes. During the 2006 parliamentary elections, his Party of Regions earned the most votes and Yanukovych won a second term as Prime Minister (2006-2007).

The Orange Revolution made the general public more interested in politics and political satire became all the rage. 'At first, it was mostly the KVN fans who came to the shows,' recalled actor Valeriy Zhidkov. 'But by the second one, half the Ukrainian parliament was there.'

Vecherniy Kvartal spared nobody. In Zelensky's sketches, the 'Dear friends' with which Yushchenko always started his speeches became a standard euphemism for the President's business associates who were lining their pockets – despite Yushchenko's solemn election pledge to put an end to corruption.

Various politicians tried to buy out Zelensky. 'They would often call, with a proposition to "collaborate" under favourable financial conditions,' said Zelensky in 2008. 'But that would have compromised our work. We have never accepted even a cent to write a joke. And we never will. If we were to side with one political camp, we would be destroyed by the other.'

On the posters for a tour through Crimea in 2007, Kvartal took advantage of the persistent rumours of political interference. The credits on the poster read: 'Director – Yulia Tymoshenko,' and 'Producer: Viktor Yanukovych.'

In largely Russian-speaking Crimea, there was a major following for the Party of Regions. In the Kvartal shows, Oleksander Pikalov walked on stage as Yanukovych: 'The President of Ukraine – according to the Crimeans!' Zelensky followed as Yushchenko: 'The President of Ukraine – according to himself!'

In the show titled *The Hidden Powers Behind Kvartal 95*, Yushchenko, Yanukovych and Tymoshenko fought over who had the comedy team in their back pocket. 'That dude really takes the mickey out of me,' Yanukovych laughed. Then suddenly his face darkened: 'Say, you wouldn't happen to have his address would you?' A short time later, Yanukovych cheerfully suggested 'giving Zelensky a good roughing up.'

Censorship was not a problem in Ukraine, unlike in Russia. In 2002, Putin banned the hit series *Kukly* ('Puppets'), a Russian adaptation of the hard-hitting British political series *Spitting Image*. The President of the Russian Federation did not consider himself fair game for comedy.

In Ukraine, not everybody appreciated Kvartal's sketches. Zelensky's father believed that his son went too far. Zelensky's mother, Rymma, commented in 2013: 'The whole time he [Oleksander] would say: "Stop making jokes about our

President."' Oleksander Zelensky grew up with the dogmas of the Communist Party, and in the east of the country especially, the notion of a holy, sacrosanct leader was still common currency. In 2009, the economics newspaper, *Kommersant,* asked the director of the theatre in Donetsk which show should be axed straight away. '*Vecherniy Kvartal,*' replied Vadym Pysaryev without hesitation. 'I have never been a fan of the orange side [Yushchenko], but the way *Vecherniy Kvartal* portrays the President... it's scandalous.'

In western Ukraine, too, there was some discontent about the group's portrayal of Yushchenko. In 2008, Zelensky revealed that the nationalists used their influence in government to have *Vecherniy Kvartal* taken off-air. 'You don't need to be a nationalist to stand behind the nation,' Zelensky explained. 'Thankfully people understand that we are creating a national product and that we are citizens of this country, even though we make jokes in Russian.'

Not all of the jokes were political in nature. 'I never believed that we were making a political show,' said Zelensky in 2013. 'Political satire never made up more than 10 per cent of the material.' Many of the sketches on *Vecherniy Kvartal* presented relatable situations from everyday life in Ukraine: alcoholism, corrupt traffic police, or arguments with the wife after a night out with the boys.

Kvartal was not averse to clichés or stereotypes. 'Us men simply don't understand women,' said Zelensky during a performance. Kvartal colleague Yuriy Krapov nodded in agreement: 'Only a woman will travel all over town to find potatoes that are 50 cents cheaper, then take a taxi home because they're so heavy.'

The shows were lightened up with appearances by popular Ukrainian and Russian pop stars. Each performance ended with an original song by Kvartal, a wistful reflection on life in Ukraine. With laughter, tears, and political satire for the broadest possible audience, *Vecherniy Kvartal* was a genuine, all-round comedy sensation.

Vecherniy Kvartal was the first commercial success for Studio Kvartal 95, the production company founded jointly by Zelensky and the Shefir brothers. The contract with Inter required Kvartal 95 to make eight shows per year, for which the television station paid them US$40,000-50,000 per episode. They also received US$150,000-200,000 for every full house at Kyiv's Ukraïna theatre. And just like in the KVN days, Kvartal 95 was always on tour throughout the country. The average takings per provincial gig totalled around US$15,000. In 2006, the young Zelensky family went on a holiday abroad for the first time.

A documentary in 2013 showed Kvartal 95 travelling in a bus for hour upon hour across Ukraine's rough asphalt. As various members of the troupe lay asleep in the back of the bus, Zelensky was on the phone. When not on a call, he spent time selecting the movies to be shown during the bus rides. The members of Kvartal 95 already knew almost all of them by heart. 'It's always me who buys the DVDs,' said Zelensky. 'I don't understand why the others never do.'

Kvartal 95 only ever had one boss. Zelensky worked an 80-hour week, and expected the same dedication from his fellow members. Half-hearted rehearsals were not an option. The Ukrainian media wrote that Zelensky was a perfectionist, and dealt out a tongue-lashing when other actors forgot their lines. He called it his 'natural authority.' 'I'm always ready to have a firm word with anyone.' Zelensky himself found criticism hard to deal with. 'It stays with me a long time, and I obsess about it a lot.'

Whenever the Kvartal actors were late to a rehearsal, Zelensky imposed a penalty. 'He's become stricter,' said Olena Kravets in an interview in 2010. 'Vova is a workaholic, he's in a constant state of elevated activity and drive. When you're like that, it's impossible to be soft on other people.'

'I have no time for pleasantries,' Zelensky responded. 'But I love my team, and I can only hope they forgive me for it.'

Zelensky's heavy-handedness was mitigated somewhat by his loyalty. The Kvartal 95 business made payments and provided the collateral for the actors' mortgages, which suddenly put a house within reach of its members. 'The greatest asset of Kvartal 95 is its people,' said Zelensky, 'and they are greatly appreciated.' Since 1997, only one performer has ever left the group, Denys Manzhosov. Zelensky had little to say about his departure.

In 2004, another star joined the Kvartal 95 constellation: Yevhen Koshovy, who came from a small village in the Luhansk region, and was the only member of Kvartal 95 ever to have studied at a proper theatre academy. From 2000 to 2005 he performed in the Luhansk-based team Va Banque. But in 2005, the towering, bald-headed Koshovy made the switch to Kvartal 95. 'A man with totally natural charisma,' said Zelensky, 'and a God-given talent.' Although Koshovy's popularity rivalled Zelensky's own, there was no jealousy between the two men, and they became friends for life.

Vecherniy Kvartal became one of the most successful shows in Ukrainian television history.

Zelensky rented office space close to the centre of Kyiv, and within a few years, the company occupied multiple floors in a premises on Belarus Street. A potential move to Moscow, where most Ukrainian entertainers earned their money, was out of the question. 'Life is pleasant and comfortable in Kyiv,' Zelensky said. 'Especially since all my colleagues and people on my wavelength live here.'

In 2010, Studio Kvartal 95 had 50 employees: 10 actors, 26 writers, and additional support staff. The creative process ran with almost military precision. One group of workers would spend the day trawling the internet to discover what people were talking about – finding out what was hot, and what was not. Once the reconnaissance was complete and the scouts reported back, Zelensky and the writers started thinking about the jokes with the actors. The creative and business director of the company always kept people around him, as a sounding board for ideas. 'I don't do well on my own,' Zelensky explained. 'I get bored. To me, it is essential to working together to come up with ideas.' Zelensky was a great motivator, but admitted himself that he was not a good manager – he was too chaotic. Still, he refused to hire a personal assistant. Because he was constantly at work, he ate a lot of junk food and had no time for exercise. He had also been a heavy smoker since his youth.

Zelensky's ultimate dream was always to make movies, but his first success as a producer was with a TV series. The sitcom *Svaty* ('The In-Laws') is about two elderly married couples, who fight for the attention of Zhenya, their only grandchild. Grandparents Ivan and Valentina come from a small village, while Yuriy and Olga are urban intellectuals. The idea for the series was born when Zelensky started talking to his script writers about his own parents and in-laws, though the scenarios were familiar to everybody in the former Soviet Union. Take the scene when Zhenya's mother calls Valentina to organise a babysitter for the holidays:

'Hi mum, we're going to Italy.'
'But... why?'

The first season of *Svaty* – which was actually two short television films – was shot in 2008, using both Ukrainian and Russian actors. And though it was a raging success, it was not exactly profitable. Zelensky spent US$250,000 to US$300,000 on each episode. *Svaty* did not gain real traction until the Russian state broadcaster Rossiya purchased the series in 2009. 'Russia is an enormous market, and that will allow us to make good-quality television,' Zelensky said. Meanwhile, Ukrainian TV companies were lining up to invest in Kvartal 95. In 2008, Inter's CEO, Valeriy Khoroshovskyi, purchased 50 per cent of the shares in Studio Kvartal 95. The Ukrainian edition of Forbes estimated the purchase at US$12 million.

Svaty had such high ratings, it was nominated for the Most Popular Sitcom award at the Festival de Télévision in Monte Carlo. The two other nominees were the American hit series *Desperate Housewives* and *The Big Bang Theory*. During the award ceremony, Prince Albert II of Monaco and *Desperate Housewives* star Eva Longoria had front-row seats, while Zelensky and his wife – decked out in a tuxedo and evening gown – were chased off the red carpet by security: who were these unknown Ukrainians? Zelensky himself found the story hilarious, and still relishes telling it in great detail.

In 2009, Zelensky realised his dream and produced a movie for cinema. The scenario for the romantic comedy *Love in the Big City* was originally conceived for Kyiv, but Zelensky was unable to secure a Ukrainian investor. The Russian firm that was prepared to advance the US$3.5 million in production costs had no interest in filming in the Ukrainian capital – why not go to New York instead? Zelensky played the lead role, and nearly all of the other actors were Russian. 'If only Ukrainians were prepared to invest in film, then the profits would stay in the country and the Ukrainian film sector could flourish,' said Zelensky. Though not exactly an artistic triumph, *Love in the Big City* was a commercial success and the beginning of a whole series of romantic comedies, all starring Zelensky in the lead role.

Studio Kvartal 95 thus blossomed into an empire, a comedy factory specialising in comical productions. Between 2003 and 2022, the company made 10 movies, four documentaries, 40 films for television, and 17 other programmes. In the meantime, *Vecherniy Kvartal* continued to perform throughout the country. As if that wasn't enough, in late 2010 Zelensky was made a producer at Inter – or 'creative director,' as he preferred to call himself. Wasting no time, he immediately came up with 30 new formats. Inter was over the moon with its new creative dynamo, but less so with the annual figures. Zelensky the perfectionist spent far too much on all the programmes.

By then, Zelensky was a force to be reckoned with. In 2011 he presented *The X Factor* for Russian television, alongside Russian singers and superstars Filipp Kirkorov and Alla Pugacheva. Volodymyr Zelensky, the provincial Ukrainian from Kryvyi Rih, had become a household name in Russia. But his relationship with Russia was more a marriage of convenience: 'To be honest, we're getting a bit sick of all those Russian stars,' Zelensky let slip during an interview in 2013. 'We want to show people that there is enough Ukrainian talent as well.'

One of the greatest Ukrainian stars was Zelensky himself. In 2008, a Ukrainian glossy voted him the most attractive man in the country. But Zelensky didn't let it go to his head: 'What do they mean, the most attractive man? They just chose someone popular. I'm not unhappy with my looks. But I'm a comic actor, and for comedians, looks aren't that important.'

In 2013, Volodymyr and Olena had a second child, a son. Kyrylo was Christened in the church of St. Elijah in Kyiv, the oldest orthodox church of Rus'. According to one society newspaper, Zelensky's parents were 'unable' to attend the ceremony.

Over the preceding years, Zelensky's daughter, Sasha, had fallen into the background. 'I hardly ever see my daughter,' he said in 2010, 'because I never have a day off.' To make any time for Olena and his children, Zelensky sacrificed a lot. 'I never go off and do anything without them, no Friday afternoon beers with the boys, no clubbing.' In 2013, Zelensky said: 'I try to spend some time with the family every night. But even 10 minutes is a bonus. I work 24 hours a day.'

In 2008, Zelensky bought a house in Ivankovychi, an exclusive, fenced-in residential area 35km south of Kyiv. The Shefir brothers lived next door. Zelensky and his colleagues often went on holiday together, with the whole family. 'Every time, I have to promise that I won't drag everybody off on excursions,' Zelensky said in 2011. 'The plan is always to lie on the beach and sunbathe... and what do you think always happens? Everyone gets a tan on the beach while I go off exploring on my own.'

Meanwhile, the Orange coalition of President Yushchenko and Tymoshenko had fallen apart. The presidential elections in February 2010 were easy pickings for Viktor Yanukovych, the chosen representative of the Donetsk clan. Yushchenko polled only five per cent of the votes.

Ukrainians were disappointed: over the previous five years, the departing head of state had failed to enact reforms and fulfil his anti-corruption promises. Yanukovych had no such intentions, and under his leadership, funds were syphoned away from the state at an unprecedented rate, even by Ukrainian standards. The greatest culprit was Yanukovych himself.

The new President immediately set about centralising power. Although the Ukrainian constitution states that coalitions may only be formed from existing parties in the Rada, Yanukovych forged a majority through the bribery and intimidation of individual parliamentary members. The new coalition forced Yanukovych's biggest opponent, Yulia Tymoshenko, to step down as Prime Minister. Next, Yanukovych fired all Yushchenko-appointed administrators, and had the Constitutional Court repeal an amendment that had been introduced during the Orange Revolution, thus granting the President more powers. Step by step, the President brought courts under his political control, and the press was subjected to censorship. During Yanukovych's presidency, the independent American non-profit organisation Freedom House altered its assessment of Ukraine from 'free' to 'partly free.'

Under the banner of 'anti-corruption,' Yanukovych began persecuting his political opponents, starting with Tymoshenko. An initial lawsuit charging her with the 'illegal' allocation of IMF funds came to nothing. But the President was determined. In the winter of 2009-2010, the annual gas-pricing negotiations between Russia and Ukraine – in which Tymoshenko represented Ukraine – had escalated into a major conflict. To eliminate his opponent once and for all, Yanukovych had the Public Prosecutor's Office instigate legal proceedings against the former prime minister due to 'abuse of powers' during those negotiations. In 2011, a Kyiv court loyal to Yanukovych sentenced Tymoshenko to seven years in prison – a verdict denounced by the EU. The former Minister of the Interior, Yuriy Lutsenko, was also imprisoned.

In an attempt to win votes in the east leading up to the parliamentary elections, in 2012 Yanukovych increased the status of the Russian language. From then on, regional parliaments were legally permitted to introduce a second 'regional' language in addition to Ukrainian, which would be certified for use in government communications and by the judiciary. The new law encouraged other minority languages (such as Hungarian), but it was primarily used by regions of south-eastern Ukraine to reintroduce Russian for government communication – to the fury of the opposition.

On 9th July 2011, Yanukovych turned 61, and his lavish birthday celebrations were lifted by appearances from well-known performers. The evening's hostess was a Russian socialite and presenter, Ksenia Sobchak. Zelensky also made an appearance, in exchange for a hefty fee. Journalists estimated that the celebrity appearances cost around US$330,000 (still less than the US$450,000 that Yanukovych is rumoured to have spent on a golden toilet.)

The President was also willing to open the treasury to Kvartal 95. In 2018, Zelensky revealed that Yanukovych had offered him US$100 million for political control of *Vecherniy Kvartal* and other programmes. Zelensky refused. On three occasions he was summoned to the presidential palace, and each time Yanukovych asked whether Zelensky might consider expressing himself 'with greater caution.' Zelensky found the meetings intimidating, and would later speak of a 'difficult moment' in his life.

'Every time, I explained my position: I cannot work under strict censorship. If that were ever the case, I would have no choice but to close Kvartal 95 for good. I said to him: "If we have to shut up shop, then I'll have to go to the press and hope for a show of support." Yanukovych replied: "Oh no, that seems like a bad idea... shutting up shop... no, I've changed my mind."'

4. Maidan

On 11th December 2013, Kvartal presented its usual New Year's gala show. This time, however, the events of the preceding weeks had forced Zelensky and his colleagues to rewrite their material dozens of times.

Nine years after the first Maidan revolution, protesters had once again pitched camp on Independence Square in Kyiv. This time, rather than stolen elections, the issue was whether Ukraine should continue charting a course towards the West, or seek closer ties to Russia. At the last minute, President Yanukovych had called off signing a much-discussed EU Association Agreement, and the protesters were demanding that he either change his mind and sign the agreement after all, or step down as President.

On 30th November, Yanukovych gave the order for the Ukrainian riot police – the Berkut – to clear out the Maidan. Brute

Euromaidan protests: *Demonstrators gather in Maidan Square in Kyiv to protest against President Yanukovych.*
Nessa Gnatoush, CCBY2.0, via Wikimedia Commons

force was applied, and the images of the riot squad descending on the unarmed demonstrators shocked the nation, further fuelling the protests. On the night of 10th December, the Berkut attacked once again and this time the protesters fought back.

Zelensky was worried that nobody would come to the show, but the 4,000-seat auditorium was nearly sold out.

'Four thousand people in the centre of Kyiv, and no Berkut to be seen,' Zelensky quipped. 'What a nice change.' The audience laughed, and the tension was broken.

As always, Kvartal did nothing to sugar-coat reality. The curtain was raised to reveal a line of riot police, standing in a semi-circle behind their shields.

'Our nation has a tradition,' said the announcer. 'Every 10 years, around New Year, people gather on Independence Square to set important change in motion and make an important decision: either six of one, or half a dozen of the other.'

The semi-circle broke, revealing a richly-laden table at which sat two men: former President Viktor Yushchenko (Zelensky), and President Viktor Yanukovych (Oleksander Pikalov). They had been ideological opponents during the 2004 Orange Revolution, but afterwards they joined forces and politics in Ukraine became business-as-usual. Zelensky framed the two politicians as members of the same corrupt in-club.

A helmeted Berkut officer pours vodka and Yanukovych raises his glass: 'Let us drink a toast.'

At that moment, former world boxing champion Vitali Klitschko (played by Yuriy Koryavchenkov) appears on stage – one of the leaders of the ongoing Maidan protests.

'Vitali, what are you doing in here?' Yanukovych asks. 'Why aren't you out on the front line?'

'I'm not going,' replies Klitschko.

'Hmm, yes, you probably don't want to hit anybody,' says Yushchenko empathetically, but Klitschko shakes his head. 'I have one golden rule in life: I only hit people for money.'

Opposition leader Arseniy Yatsenyuk (Yuriy Krapov) enters. Since Yulia Tymoshenko has been in prison for two years, Yatsenyuk is now head of the Fatherland party.

'I, Yatsenyuk, am leader of the opposition!' he calls out through his megaphone. 'People, rise up!' 'Say something about Yulia!' Klitschko whispers hoarsely.

Yatsenyuk lowers the megaphone. 'Let's just leave her where she is for the moment.'

Many Ukrainian celebrities made an appearance on the Maidan. One of them, the European Song Festival winner Ruslana, declared that she would 'set herself on fire' if necessary, if the Government did not take immediate action. A rock star, Svyatoslav Vakarchuk, and his band, Okean Elzy, warmed the hearts of the protesters, who had already been camping in the snow for weeks. Although their song 'I won't give up without a fight' was originally a love song, it ultimately grew into a battle cry for the 'Euromaidan.'

While other Ukrainian stars played an express part in the protests, Zelensky remained non-partisan and did not perform on Independence Square. 'We communicate via *Vecherniy Kvartal*,' Zelensky said. 'I am keen to demonstrate, but my support is for the people, not for promises by the Government or the opposition.'

In truth, President Yanukovych would have preferred not to have to choose between east and west. Since his election in 2010, the Donbas politician had maintained former President Kuchma's strategy for foreign policy: to serve two masters, and butter one's bread on both sides. Yanukovych sought ties with Europe, while simultaneously showing interest in joining the customs union of Russia, Belarus and Kazakhstan – a project that Putin believed could grow into a counterpart to the EU, the 'Eurasian Union.' In the past, playing this kind of double-game had always worked in Ukraine's favour, furnishing the country with both European subsidies on the one hand and discounted Russian gas on the other.

But Yanukovych was broke. He and his business associates (known throughout the country as 'the family') had spent the last four years pillaging the national treasury of the poorest country in Europe. Since Yanukovych's appointment in 2010, at least US$44 billion worth of state assets had disappeared. The thievery of Yanukovych and 'the family' was so great, in fact, that nothing was left for general expenses – at a time when the country's economic growth had fallen to 0 per cent.

Yanukovych had already approached the International Monetary Fund, but IMF loans are subject to strict criteria, such as a review of Government finances and far-reaching economic reforms – measures that would have spelled the end for Yanukovych and his cronies. President Putin threw him a lifeline: if the Ukrainian President were willing to join the Russian customs union, Yanukovych would receive a US$15 billion loan, and a sizeable rebate on gas prices.

In defence of this deal, Yanukovych tried to convince his own people that collaboration with the EU would have a negative impact on the economy – price hikes and unemployment, to be specific. To the EU itself, Yanukovych used geopolitical arguments. 'I stood up to the Russian behemoth alone for three-and-a-half years,' the Ukrainian President said to German Chancellor Angela Merkel. The remark was made on 28th November 2013 at a summit in Vilnius, where the European Association Agreement was supposed to have been signed. Yanukovych symbolically held up both fists together.

But many Ukrainians refused to sit back while their country was sold out from under them. According to polls, at least half of the population was in favour of EU membership. Now, suddenly, their country was in danger of drifting right back into the Russian sphere of influence. The west of the country was especially furious. The divide between the east and the west, between the Party of Regions and the opposition, between fostering closer ties with Moscow or charting a pro-European course, suddenly seemed insurmountable. When Kvartal member Oleksander Pikalov – who always played the President – went to show solidarity with the protesters, an unpleasant surprise awaited him. 'They all suddenly let loose at me, as though I were the real Yanukovych.'

By the New Year, the centre of Kyiv looked like a war zone. On Independence Square, dissidents with helmets and shields manned barricades several metres high. Every day saw skirmishes with the Berkut. Volunteers made Molotov cocktails, doctors cared for the injured, and car tyres burned during the ice-cold winter nights.

To put an end to the protests, Yanukovych resorted to terror. On 25th December, an investigative journalist, Tetyana Chornovol, was dragged from her car and beaten by unknown assailants. In January, two wounded activists were kidnapped from hospital, tortured and dumped in a forest outside of Kyiv. One of the two, Yuriy Verbytskyi, died from his injuries.

On 18th February 2014, the Maidan protests turned into a bloodbath when a group 20,000 strong advanced on the Parliament. The mob was held in check by the Berkut, while the city centre became a battlefield. The offices of the Party of the Regions were set alight, and the police and secret service (SBU) announced that any means to end the chaos were justified. Snipers opened fire from the rooftops, and the world was treated to footage of protesters being gunned down while huddling desperately behind their metal shields. Within the span of three days, 71 protesters and 11 police officers lost their lives. The unrelenting, senseless violence rendered Yanukovych's position untenable and dozens of his MPs left the party.

Kvartal 95 announced the cancellation of any further shows. 'Horrible things are happening in this country,' said a highly emotional Zelensky to newspaper *Komsomolskaya Pravda in Ukraine*. 'I'm ready to collapse, I'm scared and angry.' Zelensky continued to maintain his politically neutral position, however. 'What is needed to stabilise the situation in Ukraine? The four leaders of this country – the opposition leaders and the President – all need to bugger the hell off!'

Since late January, Yanukovych had been negotiating with the three opposition leaders: Arseniy Yatsenyuk (from the Fatherland party), Vitali Klitschko (leader of the Strike party) and Oleh Tyahnybok (of the right-wing nationalist Freedom party). But to no avail. While the politicians quibbled, thought Zelensky, Ukrainians were being shot dead in the centre of Kyiv:

'The people must elect new leaders, otherwise the deaths will continue. These four men are responsible for the Ukrainians who have already lost their lives.'

Victory went to the Maidan. After mediation by Germany, France and Poland, Yanukovych signed a deal with the opposition. The President was to remain in power for the time being, but he agreed to call early elections before the end of the year.

On Independence Square, the gunned-down protesters (the 'Heavenly Hundred') were processed around in coffins. That evening, Vitali Klitschko attempted to explain the deal with Yanukovych to the masses. Klitschko was booed away, and the protesters demanded Yanukovych's immediate resignation. Activists from the ultra-nationalist 'Right Sector' threatened to storm the presidential palace – during attacks on police stations in Lviv, the nationalists had acquired hundreds of firearms. That night, members of the Berkut started deserting en masse. Ministers and highly-ranked public servants also took flight. At Zhuliany airport near Kyiv, the private jets took off one after another.

On the evening of 21st February, Yanukovych left for Kharkiv, where a conference was held the following day with administrators from eastern Ukraine and Crimea titled 'Stop Maidan.' The attendees decided that local authorities should no longer listen to Kyiv. Not everybody in Kharkiv agreed, however: during the meetings, hundreds of enraged Maidan supporters protested before the conference centre.

When Yanukovych saw the tense situation in Kharkiv, he became afraid and flew to Donetsk to seek support from the billionaire oligarch Rinat Akhmetov. But even the country's richest resident believed that the President should resign. In desperation, Yanukovych attempted to seek refuge in Russia, but air traffic control at the local airport refused to allow his jet to leave. Ultimately, Russian commandos (*spetsnaz*) took the deposed President by car to a Russian marine base in Crimea. From there, he made his way to Russia.

Once Yanukovych's escape became known, the (now severely depleted) Verkhovna Rada called an emergency session. In a vote of 328 to none (with six abstentions), the Parliament voted out the President of Ukraine. That same day, the Parliament also voted for the immediate release of Yulia Tymoshenko, and members of her Fatherland party were assigned key Government positions. Oleksander Turchynov was appointed interim President, and party leader Arseniy Yatsenyuk became Prime Minister of the new Government. The next day, the Rada also voted to repeal the law granting Russian 'regional administrative language' status.

While the Maidan movement celebrated, eastern Ukraine saw almost daily protests against the Maidan uprising. Demonstrators in Kharkiv and Donetsk demanded autonomy, and some waved Russian flags.

The Kremlin was deeply disillusioned with Yanukovych's sudden departure. Over the previous weeks, Russia had done its utmost to keep the Ukrainian President in power. On 20th and 21st February, FSB general Sergey Beseda (now chief of the Fifth Department of Foreign Intelligence) was in Kyiv as an adviser, and President Putin telephoned Yanukovych nearly every day. The crisis in Ukraine ruined the jubilant atmosphere of the Sochi Winter Olympics, where Russia – aided by large-scale doping – won most of the medals. Putin could have killed Yanukovych. According to the investigative journalist, Mikhail Zygar, in a rage Putin called Yanukovych an 'unimaginable scumbag and a coward.'

On the evening of 22nd February, the Russian President summoned the security council to his Moscow residence. The crisis meeting went on all night. 'It finished at around seven in the morning,' Putin later recalled. 'As we all left, I said to my colleagues: "We must take immediate action to bring Crimea back to Russia."'

Five days later, Russian special forces occupied the local parliament in Simferopol. Armed men in camouflage chased parliamentarians into the plenary hall, where they voted in a referendum on the surrender of Crimea. Military units appeared on the streets throughout the peninsula. Russian soldiers – without insignia – took control of strategic locations, such as train stations, police stations and administrative buildings. Ukrainian army bases were surrounded.

'Little green men': *Russian troops occupy the Crimea in 2014.*
Anton Holoborodko, CCBY-SA 3.0 via Wikimedia Commons

For days, the Kremlin claimed to have no knowledge of who these 'green men' were who had invaded Crimea. 'Walk into a store in Russia, and you can buy any uniform you like,' was Putin's dismissive response.

On 28th February, Yanukovych gave a press conference in Rostov. The former President seemed adamant. 'I have not been deposed,' he said. 'I was forced to leave Ukraine for fear of my life, and the lives of my loved ones.' Yanukovych refused to acknowledge the new Turchynov Government. And although the refugee president said that he despised 'all forms of military interference,' he made multiple appeals to Putin, saying that 'Russia needs to take action.' His words added fuel to the fire for all the demonstrators who had taken to the streets throughout eastern Ukraine. Many Russian-speaking Ukrainians were angry at the deposition of 'their' President, and at the plans to abolish Russian as an official state language. In the provinces of Donetsk and Luhansk, many people tuned in to Russian TV channels, where there were constant reports of a 'coup' by Ukrainian nationalists and 'fascists' who were out to purge the country of ethnic Russians.

Zelensky decided that he could no longer remain on the sidelines, that he had to speak out. On 1st March, he organised a guest appearance on the news programme of 1+1, where Studio Kvartal 95 was under contract. Zelensky addressed Yanukovych directly. 'I know you personally, we've met several times,' Zelensky said. 'You are a man of strong character. Now you must be strong once more, and step aside. You are not the President any longer, the people of Ukraine have made that decision.'

Zelensky had a message for the interim Government and the Rada. 'I would also like to address those currently in power. If people in the east or in Crimea want to speak Russian, then just leave them be.'

Next he turned to President Putin, whose 'men in green' stood face-to-face with Ukrainian soldiers in Crimea. 'Dear Vladimir Vladimirovich, please avoid even the smallest hint of a military conflict. I will get down on my knees and beg, if necessary.'

The war came regardless. On 16th March, the Crimean population voted to join the Russian Federation, with a North Korean-style majority of 96.7 per cent. Independent observers identified signs of large-scale manipulation at the polling booths. On 18th March, Putin signed the documents that officially annexed Crimea to the Russian Federation.

But things did not end there. On 6th April, a protest in Donetsk city centre ended in an occupation of the Regional State Administration building. The protesters took shelter behind barricades, and announced the inception of the Donetsk People's Republic. The square in front of the administrative building was patrolled by aggressive thugs wearing leather jackets. The police were nowhere to be seen.

On 12th April, Russian ex-soldier and FSB officer, Igor Girkin, and around 80 armed civilians occupied the city of Sloviansk in the north of Donetsk province. Girkin, alias Strelkov ('shooter'), was a nationalist with an imperialist worldview. By occupying the city, he hoped to trigger an uprising in the Donbas that would lead to the Russian conquest of Novorossia, the old tsarist designation for south-eastern Ukraine. In other cities, too, armed separatists took control, many of whom had served in the Soviet army, such as Igor Bezler ('Bes') in Horlivka. Others had a Russian passport, such as Alexander Borodai, who was appointed Prime Minister of the Donetsk People's Republic in May. Phone conversations tapped by the Ukrainian secret service, the SBU, revealed that Girkin and Borodai were in contact with the Russian Government.

An armed conflict ultimately became inevitable, and acting President Turchynov mobilised the Ukrainian army, announcing an Anti-Terrorist Operation. On 13th April, Ukrainian troops surrounded Sloviansk. When separatists attempted to occupy the police station in nearby Kramatorsk, shots were fired from both sides. Ukrainian armoured personnel carriers drove on the roads of the Donbas region, and fighter aircraft circled in the skies.

It was under these conditions that Kvartal 95 toured through eastern Ukraine with a new programme. On 15th April Zelensky performed in Donetsk, and on 17th April the group travelled on to nearby Horlivka. Before the Donetsk performance, Zelensky gave an interview to the local press.

'Weren't you frightened to come to the Donbas, with the current civil unrest?' one journalist asked.

'Our families are worried,' Zelensky answered, 'but they also thought it was important for us to bring some humour. We've come to cheer people up. We'll see later on whether the venue is booked out.'

Zelensky was asked whether he saw any way out of the crisis.

'The only thing we can do for Ukraine right now is to call for unity,' was his response.

Zelensky was still convinced that the unrest in the east and the annexation of Crimea were attributable to the ongoing political conflicts and division in his country. 'If we can finally learn to love one another, then believe me, nobody will want to separate,' he had already said earlier. The performances in Donetsk and Horlivka were a gesture of reconciliation.

That night, the Palace of Children and Youth Creativity in Donetsk was nearly sold out. Kvartal had adapted the evening's programme somewhat. The sketch in which the Cossacks write a letter to Putin – a reference to the famed (but apocryphal) 17th Century letter of reprimand to the Ottoman sultan – was scrapped, and replaced by other material. Oleh Tyahnybok (played by Zelensky) from the ultra-right Freedom party appeared on stage, and let out the old nationalist cry that had become common since the Maidan revolution: '*Slava Ukraini!*' (Glory to Ukraine!)

'Oleh, have you gone completely mad? We're in Donetsk!'

But Zelensky does not want merely please the crowd. 'It actually wouldn't be so bad if Putin became President of Ukraine,' he says. 'Then at least Crimea would be ours again.'

That night, Kvartal sang a melancholic song about the annexation, a cover version of a hit song by Russian singer Alla Pugacheva about lost love. In Zelensky's version, Crimea is the lover who has gone off with someone else. Though no recording survives of the performance in Donetsk, Zelensky did reprise the song at a later performance, with tears in his eyes:

One day you will return to me,
Unable to bear the weapons and the outright lies.
I believe it so strongly
That I spend all day waiting by the door.

On 25th May, with Independence Square still looking like a military campsite, early presidential elections were held. After the first round, there was already a clear winner: Petro Poroshenko, a billionaire who had made his fortune in confectionery and baked goods. Ukraine thus elected an oligarch with a long career in politics, but voted expressly against the Fatherland party that had come to power through the Maidan movement. Yulia Tymoshenko obtained only 12.8 per cent of the vote. Zelensky voted for Poroshenko, as did his parents, who were formerly Yanukovych supporters.

Poroshenko was placed at the helm of a bankrupt country. He recalled: 'When I became President – and I kid you not – our treasury had US$4000 in cash, US$5 billion worth of gold reserves, and a US$7.5 billion national debt to be repaid within several months.' In addition to the disastrous finances, battles with armed separatists were also escalating. The Ukrainian army was in such a sorry state that the Government resorted to volunteer regiments that were being formed all over the country. Among the volunteers were many nationalists, including radicals from the Right Sector. The Russian Government propaganda referred to them 'Nazis' and 'Einsatzgruppen,' bent on the extermination of the Russian-speaking Donbas population. In reality, large swathes of Russian-speaking Ukrainians also took up arms to defend their country. In June, Poroshenko gave the green light for a major offensive, and the separatists in the Donetsk People's Republic and the neighbouring Luhansk Republic were gradually driven back.

In May, Zelensky had started filming *8 New Dates*, the sequel to the romantic comedy *8 First Dates*. It was once again a Ukrainian-Russian collaboration, starring both well-known Ukrainian and Russian actors. Between shoots, the artistic director still found time to appear on Kvartal 95's own show, *Only News*, where he made jokes from the Red Square about Putin. Zelensky could see how the annexation of Crimea had led to euphoria in Russia, where the state media had used the slogan 'Crimea is Ours' to whip up national hysteria – to Zelensky's great frustration. He got into arguments with his Russian friends, such as Alexander Chadov. 'He told me in a restaurant that Crimea was theirs. I flew into such a rage, they had to call the police,' Zelensky later recalled.

In the Donbas, the separatists lost more and more ground. Igor Girkin was forced to give up Sloviansk and flee to Donetsk, where he proclaimed himself Minister of Defence. In desperation, Girkin called Sergey Aksyonov, whom Russia had appointed 'Head of the Crimean Republic,' saying that Moscow should send more weaponry: tanks, artillery, and heavy air-defence systems. On 17th July, A Malaysia Airlines Boeing 777 on the way from Amsterdam to Kuala Lumpur was shot down above eastern Ukraine by a Russian Buk anti-aircraft missile. All 298 people on board lost their lives. The attack – with so many victims from the West – made it clear to the world at a single stroke that Ukraine was at war, and also who was responsible for the violence. The next day, Washington publicly announced that the rocket had been fired from the region occupied by the pro-Russian separatists, and the West introduced a new round of economic sanctions against Russia.

Moscow was not ready to concede victory to Kyiv, however. When the Ukrainian army threatened to surround Donetsk, the Russian army crossed the border – again wearing unmarked uniforms. In August, the Ukrainians were surrounded at Ilovaisk and hundreds were killed.

One sultry evening in August, Kvartal 95 performed at the front in Kramatorsk, to an audience of exhilarated soldiers. Olena Kravets was initially hesitant to go to the Donbas, but allowed herself to be convinced. Kvartal member Stepan Kazanin – a Russian citizen – also appeared. Some 'serious discussions' were held within the group when the war initially broke out, but Kvartal 95 had since closed ranks again.

On a makeshift stage, with a backdrop of black plastic, Kvartal ended their performance in the usual manner, with a nostalgic song:

I love my Fatherland, it's true,
Though oft I've gone in search of more.
But north or south, from east to west,
My brothers, never would I split it apart.

(...)

But what's a fatherland to me?
A cold step-parent, or a loving mother?
Perhaps we should set our differences aside.
All I want is to live in peace and harmony.

Kvartal 95 performed all along the front lines: not only in Kramatorsk, but also in Sloviansk and Mariupol. The performances had a profound effect on Zelensky. Like most Ukrainians, he had always looked down on the military, with their rigid discipline and sadistic initiation rituals for new recruits. But the soldiers he met on the front lines were totally different, Zelensky said during an interview: 'If these types of people were to form the basis for a new Ukrainian army, you would have no problem sending your kids off to military service. I met real men, who endured tremendous hardships but still managed to hold on to their humanity.'

Because the Ukrainian army was so under-resourced, many Ukrainians provided financial support for the purchase of uniforms, boots and rations. Zelensky also donated. For a long time he had attempted to reconcile east with west, defending Russian as a language and expressing understanding for the separatists in the Donbas. But after his performance for the military, he finally showed his true colours. He called out to the military: 'Thank you all for defending our country against this scum.'

'I have always regarded myself as a Ukrainian national, but never have I felt like a Ukrainian deep inside,' Zelensky said to a journalist in October. 'I always wanted to be a citizen of the world, able to live and work anywhere. Now, the citizens of Ukraine have truly become Ukrainians.'

In Russia, Zelensky's support for the Ukrainian army did not go unnoticed. In the Russian media, his Moscow showbiz colleagues discussed how he could have sunk so low. Russian parliamentarians accused him of having sponsored Ukrainian 'death squads' to the tune of US$75,000. The Russian Public Prosecutor's Office opened a lawsuit against him.

In December, *8 New Dates* premiered in Moscow without Zelensky. The director of Studio Kvartal 95 had no interest in attending. Slowly but surely, Studio Kvartal 95 lost its business in Russia, which was a harsh blow to Zelensky's commercial empire.

Several years later, in 2018, a Ukrainian interviewer, Dmytro Hordon, asked Zelensky about it: 'Did the fact that you behaved like a decent human being cost you much money?'

Zelensky's response was open: 'In a commercial sense, absolutely. We used to earn US$150,000-200,000 per broadcast hour of a TV series. Once we stopped working with Russia, that amount was never higher than US$30,000.'

Hordon nodded.

'But to be honest, it doesn't worry me in the slightest,' Zelensky went on. 'Not one bit.'

5. Servant of the People

In August 2017, a well-known YouTuber, Anatoliy Yatsechko, entered the 1+1 studio premises. It was a sweltering summer's day and he and the cameraman both wore shorts.

The make-up van was dark and cool. Yatsechko was welcomed by a Kvartal actor, Yevhen Koshovy, wearing a shirt and tie. Shooting was about to start for the new season of the hit series *Servant of the People*, in which an ordinary history teacher, Vasyl Holoborodko (played by Volodymyr Zelensky), becomes President of Ukraine. Koshovy played the Minister of Foreign Affairs.

After Zelensky, Koshovy was Kvartal 95's biggest star and shared a van with his boss and best friend. 'Those are Vova's things,' he says, as Yatsechko sinks into the make-up chair.

'What about this?' the vlogger asks, triumphantly holding a up a small book to the camera: *A Hundred Short Lessons in Ukrainian*. 'Is this his, too?'

'Uh, yeah,' says Koshovy, but then has second thoughts. 'Actually, I think that really belongs to all of us.'

Like Koshovy, Volodymyr Zelensky is Russian-speaking. He only studied Ukrainian at school, and Kvartal 95's shows were almost exclusively in Russian. Although Zelensky understood Ukrainian perfectly well, his active command of the language was average, and not enough to carry a conversation.

Though initially not a big issue, it had become a major problem. The Maidan uprising of 2014 and the outbreak of war in eastern Ukraine had led to a wave of patriotism, and increased animosity toward Russia. Ukrainian was in and Russian was out. To encourage the use of Ukrainian, the Poroshenko Government had introduced a media quota stipulating that at least 75 per cent of all spoken language on television had to be in Ukrainian. Poroshenko also expedited efforts to repeal the language law introduced by Yanukovych.

Although Zelensky had already started using more Ukrainian words and expressions, he was not making real progress. He had, however, engaged the services of a teacher, he reported in the spring of 2017. Zelensky explained he was doing it 'for himself.' 'I think it's good to speak Ukrainian,' he said, then quickly slipped into comic mode: 'Soon I'll be babbling so fast, I'll be able to answer your questions before you can even ask them!'

Zelensky had also been improving himself in other areas. When his daughter Sasha came home from school one day in tears after learning that cigarettes cause cancer, he quit smoking. He also lost six kilos for his role in *Servant of the*

People, and started a rigorous exercise programme with a personal trainer. Zelensky was in his late thirties at the time, but was starting to feel his age.

In 2016, he was interviewed by the Stand-up Boys, two young YouTube comedians. 'Today, a childhood dream of Bohdan's and mine will come true!' says 20-something Serhiy Lykhovyda, a hipster with glasses and a black beard. 'We're gonna interview Volodymyr Zelensky!' adds his co-host Bohdan Gnativ, brimming with excitement.

'Jeez,' Zelensky chuckles bashfully, 'When you find out you're the childhood dream of two bearded men...'

For a long time, *Servant of the People* had also been just a dream. In 2005 Zelensky and his colleagues toyed with the notion of making a comedy series about Ukraine's abominable Government. In the initial drafts, the working title was *The Young Nation*, and the lead role was a young, idealistic politician in the provinces. 'Even then, we were eager for change,' Zelensky would later say.

The key scene from the first episode of the eventual series, which aired on 16th November 2015, made Ukrainian television history. The young history teacher, Vasyl Petrovych Holoborodko, is teaching a lesson, when the manual skills teacher comes in to collect the whole class for an odd job: voting booths need to be assembled and posters put up on the walls in preparation for the elections in a week's time. 'Come on then, move it,' the manual skills teacher says to the class.

The situation is a very familiar one to Ukrainian viewers. These types of 'public-service' jobs are always scheduled during lessons that are deemed superfluous.

'What's going on?' Holoborodko asks. 'I'm in the middle of a lesson.'

'Headmistress's orders.'

'Why can't 10A do it?'

'10A has maths right now.'

'So? I'm teaching history!'

The teacher gives him a pitying look. 'Come on, you know that's hardly the same.'

Vasyl Holoborodko erupts into blind fury. 'So history is worthless, is it? Then tell me: why do politicians keep making the same mistakes over and over again?'

'Petrovych,' is the reply, 'What's the matter?'

'I've had it. I'm bloody sick of it all,' Holoborodko rages. In the tirade that follows, all of the obscenities are tactfully bleeped out.

'You know why we all live like dogs? Because our voting starts in kennels. We've been choosing the lesser of two *bleep* for 25 years now. But you know what? This time won't be any different, and you know why? Because you, my father and I will just elect another *bleep*.'

'Vasya,' says his fellow teacher, 'Let's go have a drink, I've got a stash somewhere...'

But Holoborodko is inconsolable. 'And those *bleep* take power, and they steal *bleep* and talk *bleep*, different words, but it's all the same *bleep*. And no-one gives a flying *bleep*! Not you, not me, no-one! If I got just one week up there, I'd show them what for. *Bleep* the motorcades, *bleep* the perks, *bleep* the chalets! *Bleep* the lot of you! Let teachers live like the President, and the President like a history teacher!'

His wish is immediately granted. One of his students secretly films the tirade, and uploads it online. The video goes viral, the history teacher is asked to run in the presidential elections as an independent candidate, and wins with a majority of 67 per cent.

Various scriptwriters from Studio Kvartal 95 had a go at drafting the pivotal scene. 'But no matter who wrote it,' said writer Dmytro Grygorenko, 'it always came out about the same.'

And so – at least in the series – a new kind of leader was born. The President who cycled to work, tackled corruption, and instituted large-scale reform in Ukraine. His work was constantly undermined, not only by the actions of three sinister, anonymous oligarchs, but also by his own family, who capitalised on Vasyl's newfound status to improve their own social and financial position. *Servant of the People* not only criticises the powers-that-be, it holds up a mirror to ordinary Ukrainians.

Even from its pilot episode, the series was a ratings machine, with an average of six million Ukrainian viewers per episode (in a country of nearly 45 million inhabitants). Twenty-six per cent of the population aged between 18 and 54 tuned in to the show, which also won two major international prizes. Media giant Netflix purchased the screening rights, and film producer Fox Studios bought the 'format.' The series would see three seasons in total, along with a cinema film release.

In 2017, director Serhiy Shefir was asked to explain the enormous success of *Servant of the People*. After considering for a moment, the producer replied: 'It was an uplifting fairy tale, based on real future events – events that everybody is hoping for.'

The reality was less rosy, however.

President Poroshenko, who had won the 2014 presidential elections with a clear majority, lost the war in the east. The separatists from the self-proclaimed People's Republics of Donetsk and Luhansk had access to an endless supply of weapons, ammunition and Russian 'volunteers' – mercenaries, essentially. Moscow was prepared to send entire battalions of tanks across the border if need be, along with soldiers clothed as rebels. Moscow steadfastly denied any and all involvement in the conflict. When four Russian commandos were captured as prisoners of war in the Donbas, the Kremlin announced that the men had 'gotten lost.'

In mid-January 2015, supported by Russian military units, the separatists launched an attack on the city of Debaltseve, a major traffic hub between Donetsk and Luhansk. After a month of fighting and hundreds of casualties on both sides, the Ukrainian troops – who were all but surrounded – were forced to sound the retreat.

Debaltseve was the last major battle. Although a ceasefire had already been signed in the Belarusian capital of Minsk in September 2014, it had done nothing to stop the fighting. On 12th April 2015, Ukraine, the two Republics and Russia signed Minsk II. Shooting continued for another three days, but then the guns were silenced – for the time being.

The 'package' of measures in Minsk II included amendments to the Ukrainian constitution which allocated a 'special' autonomous status to the regions of Luhansk and Donetsk, and allowed them to elect their own representatives via local elections. In return, all armed units were required to withdraw.

Though Minsk II put an end to all-out war, it was not a basis for a long-lasting peace. The war in the Donbas simmered down to a 'frozen conflict.' The major battles had stopped, but small skirmishes continued. Fatalities and injuries – even among civilians – were still common to both sides.

Although Poroshenko was unable to end the war, he did succeed in stabilising the country, and under very difficult circumstances. The annexation of Crimea and the civil war had deprived Ukraine of large swathes of land and millions of citizens, and foreign investors were fleeing the country en masse. Between 2013 and 2015, GDP fell from US$181 billion to US$91 billion – a decline of more than 50 per cent.

After his clear victory in the first round of the 2014 presidential elections, Poroshenko had hoped for an absolute majority in the Parliament. But in the autumn of 2015, Prime Minister Yatsenyuk's People's Front party – an offshoot of Yulia Tymoshenko's Fatherland Party – garnered almost as many votes as the 'Petro Poroshenko Bloc.' Even together, the two parties could not muster a majority in the Rada.

While Poroshenko and Yatsenyuk quibbled over the ministerial posts in the new Cabinet, the American Vice-President Joe Biden took action. If the parties could not reach an agreement, Biden threatened, then the United States would cut off its financial support to Ukraine. Such a blow would cripple Kyiv, so a broad coalition of five parties that had a two-thirds majority in the Rada was formed. Yatsenyuk was re-elected as Prime Minister.

The new Government restructured the enormous national debt, and reached new loan agreements with the IMF to keep the country afloat. Poroshenko succeeded in implementing austerity measures, while simultaneously increasing defence spending from 1 to 5 per cent.

At international level, the Government was clearly charting a Western course. The annexation of Crimea and the separation of Donetsk and Luhansk had resolved the dispute between east and west Ukraine. Kyiv signed an association agreement with the EU, and applied for membership to NATO. Although the latter kept the door closed, instructors were sent in from the West to train the Ukrainian army. Poroshenko reformed his forces to conform to NATO standards, and within several years the dilapidated Ukrainian army was transformed into a robust force. After 2016, the economy also began showing signs of improvement.

But Poroshenko was a billionaire, an oligarch and a member of the old political class with his own TV channel, 5 Kanal. The 'Chocolate Prince' neglected to fulfil his election promise of selling off his confectionery empire, and also failed to effect any real change in Ukraine's corrupt political and economic structures. Poroshenko appointed the former Georgian President, Mikheil Saakashvili, a well-known anti-corruption expert, as governor of the Odessa region – historically one of the country's most mafia-heavy areas. But new faces do not guarantee genuine reform, as Oleh Rybachuk from the Ukrainian anti-corruption 'Honesty' movement said when assessing Poroshenko's first five years as President. 'He has not fulfilled the most important requirement of the Revolution of Dignity' (another name for the 2014 Maidan revolution). 'He, too, surrounds himself with corrupt figures, but closes his eyes to the fact.'

In February 2016, the 'broad coalition' fell apart, and Yatsenyuk stepped down as premier. He was succeeded by a parliamentary President, Volodymyr Hroysman, who continued to govern without a majority, necessitating the ongoing formation of ad hoc coalitions in the Rada.

Poroshenko's popularity nose-dived. In a poll from November 2017, only 16.1 per cent of respondents said they would vote for the current President. Ukraine was already looking forward to the elections scheduled for spring 2019. In October 2017, Yulia Tymoshenko announced that she was prepared to make another bid for the presidency. Others also made their intentions known.

Zelensky made his usual jokes. 'This week, with much pomp and circumstance, many representatives from our political elite have announced their plans to contend for the presidency,' he said in a Facebook video post recorded at the airport in Kyiv. 'I, Volodymyr Zelensky, aged 39 and of sound mind and body, also have an important announcement to make: I will now board my plane. Perhaps I'll even use the toilet first.'

One month later, in an interview with *Den* newspaper, the jokes had suddenly disappeared. Zelensky had 'experience' in politics, the journalist said, and more and more Ukrainians were starting to see a real president in the comic actor. Then came the question: 'Wouldn't you like to have a go at politics?'

Zelensky responded in all sincerity: 'That is a difficult question to answer, but one that is definitely worth exploring.'

In the autumn of 2017, Studio Kvartal 95 was working on the seventh season of *Svaty*, which still enjoyed enormous popularity in both Ukraine and Russia. But then, without warning, the Ukrainian secret service, the SBU, barred Russian lead Fyodor Dobronravov from entering Ukraine for three years, on the grounds that he had visited Crimea and 'showed support' for the annexation – an allegation that Dobronravov vehemently denied. Over the next few days, the Ukrainian media began issuing reports of the series potentially being axed.

The rumours were not unfounded. Although the characters in *Svaty* – two sets of grandparents squabbling over their grandchildren – represent an entire generation of Russians and Ukrainians, some took umbrage at the person of Ivan Budko, the alcoholic and short-tempered rural grandpa. Nationalistic Ukrainians had no interest in being reminded of their shared history with Russia.

'This is a pre-war series that has no place in modern Ukraine,' wrote well-known journalist Marina Danilyuk-Yarmolayeva on her Facebook page: 'Ivan Budko reflects a bygone Soviet reality, which is in no way representative of modern-day Ukraine.'

Zelensky was furious at the prospect of a ban, and spoke his mind in a Facebook video. 'This message is for the people who are dividing our country, who want to segregate us according to colour, language, and whatever else,' he said. 'I won't tell you what I really think of you – I am too civilised for that.'

Zelensky returned to the topic in his interview with *Den*, saying that he loved his work with heart and soul, and that he would not give it up 'for all the money in the world.' Still, he was considering the notion of a forced career change: 'I get the distinct impression that legislators are out to take my livelihood away from me.'

Zelensky then talked about his Kvartal colleague Stepan Kazanin, a Russian citizen who was ineligible for Ukrainian nationality. That was potentially a big problem, now that the Rada was discussing a law prohibiting all cooperation with the 'Russian aggressor.' 'So we are supposed to just send someone away who's been working with us for 15 years?' Zelensky asked out loud. 'Some of us speak Ukrainian better than some of our politicians. And who has made a greater contribution to the development of Ukrainian culture and national identity?'

He issued a warning: 'If people try to stop us doing what we love most – performing on film, TV and on stage – then I will take away their electoral support.'

Zelensky was still hesitant to admit he was planning to enter politics, but the allusions were clear.

'What kind of President does Ukraine need?' asked the journalist from *Den*.

'We just need honest people in power,' Zelensky answered. 'Sensible and honest. That's the most important thing.'

On 29th November, the troupe's fears became reality: *Svaty* was banned by the Ukrainian Ministry for Culture. Not only was it an enormous financial blow to Studio Kvartal 95, it was a sign that the Government was questioning Zelensky's loyalty. Ukraine often seems obsessed with its national identity, and in the eyes of some, making jokes about the nation was reason enough to be considered a 'traitor.'

But there were plenty of Ukrainians who felt the Government was splitting hairs. Soldiers in the field even made a video to show Zelensky their moral support. 'Volodya,' one of them said, 'Everyone at Studio Kvartal 95 is a friend to our unit. Your work has brought us joy and raised our morale. Don't worry, we're on your side!' The soldier brought his fist to his heart.

On 2nd December, Zelensky registered a political party named after the television series: Servant of the People (*Sluha Narodu*). A month later, he explained that he had done it 'just in case,' to prevent anybody else from using the name. 'This is not a genuine political project, it's more of a legal matter.'

Zelensky's switch to politics was less strange than it might seem. After 20 years he had reached the top of Ukraine's entertainment industry, while the ongoing war and the disappearance of the Russian market had made further expansion virtually impossible. At the age of 39, Zelensky was ready for a new challenge. Besides, he wanted to effect genuine change in his country. After 20 years of touring, he knew Ukraine like no other. The hit series *Servant of the People* was not just any comedy: it was Zelensky's vision for political reform.

According to Kvartal director Serhiy Shefir, Zelensky decided to run for the presidency in the spring of 2018, a decision that was taken in close consultation with the rest of Studio Kvartal 95. 'We talked about it endlessly,' Yevhen Koshovy recalled.

'Zelensky said: you do realise that everything might fall apart? I replied: if you run as a candidate, we'll make sure that Kvartal 95 doesn't fall apart.' According to Koshovy, Zelensky's wife Olena was strongly against his candidacy, but was unable to talk him out of it.

Zelensky knew he had a real chance, since he had spoken to the lawyer, politician and spin doctor Andriy Bohdan. Bohdan had shown Zelensky his polling results. 'The figures clearly showed demand for a new voice,' Bohdan recalled. 'They wanted a person from outside the system, but someone who was still well known.' Bohdan's message was clear: the voters wanted someone like Zelensky.

Bohdan himself was more a representative of the old system. For years the lawyer had been the most important adviser to the oligarch Ihor Kolomoyskyi, one of the wealthiest and most controversial figures in Ukraine. Kolomoyskyi was the founder and principal shareholder of PrivatBank, the largest bank in the country, with 20 million customers. In 2016, the bank's finances proved so precarious that the Ukrainian state came to the rescue with a bailout scheme worth billions. After that, PrivatBank was nationalised.

In 2013, Kolomoyskyi took over TV channel 1+1, where Studio Kvartal 95 was under contract. Kolomoyskyi made at least one attempt to influence Zelensky's jokes, but Zelensky paid him little heed. In his shows, Zelensky played the old oligarch as a loud-mouthed busybody, striding into the presidential office unannounced and uninvited.

Campaigner: *Zelensky plays table tennis on the
election trail in March 2019.*
IMAGO/ZUMA *Wire*

As with everything he did, Zelensky took his candidacy very
seriously. For months, Ivan Bakanov – Kvartal's legal adviser
and Zelensky's childhood friend, who had been appointed
campaign manager – helped work on strategy. In the summer
of 2018, Bakanov organised meetings with local administrators
and businesspeople, who were largely unimpressed by
Zelensky's plans: 'We were laughed at most of the time.'
Zelensky refused to be dissuaded. On the contrary, he threw
himself into his new project. By his own admission, he had over
two US$2 million to spend on his election campaign, funded
out of his own pocket and from donations from friends and

business partners. By the autumn of 2018, he was employing a sizeable campaign team.

Although Zelensky waited as long as possible to announce his candidacy in order to keep his audience in suspense, his election campaign had already begun in reality. 'The last few weeks have been a living nightmare,' he joked during an episode of *Vecherniy Kvartal* on 29th October. 'Everybody – journalists, my family – are constantly asking me one thing: are you going to run or not?'

Zelensky started going through the pros and cons of his potential candidacy with the audience. 'I have a legal background, so that's a plus. I have no experience in politics, which is... an enormous plus.'

Suddenly, his tone became serious. 'If I become President, I will of course appoint responsible people,' he said. 'The Defence minister, for example, will not be anyone who has sent soldiers to the front lines, but someone who has brought them back safely.' A silence fell in the auditorium, with a few sparse claps of approval. After four years of war, Ukrainians longed for peace.

On New Year's Eve, Zelensky officially announced his candidacy in a short video broadcast by 1+1. As a result, the traditional New Year's address by the President – Poroshenko – was pushed back, and did not air until after midnight. Responding to public criticism regarding the change of schedule, Zelensky said that it was not his idea and that there had been a 'technical error.'

Zelensky and his team were eager to shake things up with a completely new style of campaign. The comedian presented himself as the outsider coming in to clean house in Ukrainian politics, as though he were a real-life Vasyl Holoborodko. In order to reach potential voters, he made widespread use of social media.

On 2nd January, in a short video on Instagram, Zelensky called on the 'citizens of Ukraine' to join his campaign. There was only one criterion for new staff, he explained: no politicians were allowed. A little less than a week later, the presidential candidate announced that he still had no election programme. 'The old politicians are following the old recipe,' he said. 'They ask nothing, promise the world, and then fail to put it into practice. We're doing things differently: we're going to create our programme together, with your input.' Zelensky asked voters to have their say on social media, and specify what they thought were the country's five biggest problems. 'We are creating our platform in conjunction with our citizens. That is the way we will solve our problems.'

Several days later, Zelensky published a political platform titled 'The Ukraine of my Dreams.' Brimming with positive slogans, it contained little concrete policy. By clicking on the various headings, readers could leave Facebook comments and thus 'help create' the platform. The homepage sported a large photo of Zelensky as 'President' Vasyl Holoborodko. 'I want to assure you all from the outset that I intend to change the system within a single term,' he wrote in the introduction.

Zelensky's lack of any firm plans invited some criticism. After a meeting between the presidential candidate and members of the Kyiv business community, a travel agency owner, Arseniy Finberg, emerged perplexed: 'They asked him who he would appoint as chief of police and security services if he came to power. He replied, in all nonchalance: "I'll organise a national talent quest. First we'll vote on the judges, then the ministers."' Finberg's impression of Zelensky was that he 'had no idea who is responsible for what, what the presidential powers are, and what the Parliament is for.'

Just several weeks after his announcement, Zelensky nudged ahead in the polls. In late January 2019, 19 per cent of voters said they would vote for him. Yulia Tymoshenko had 18.2 per cent of the vote, and Poroshenko had 15.1 per cent. The incumbent President conducted a traditional election campaign, giving interviews and debating his political opponents. He also highlighted his role as saviour of the nation in the face of the Russian aggressors. His slogan *Armia, Mova, Vira* (Army, Language, Faith) was designed to rally support among the nationalistic and conservative powers. This approach created a large gulf in the middle of the political spectrum – a hole that Zelensky could fill.

Poroshenko was the ideal opponent for Zelensky. In an Instagram post, he addressed the incumbent President directly: 'I've finally figured out what you mean by the slogan "Army, Language, Faith": You intend to plunder the armed forces and use language to divide people, which is why faith in you is waning.'

On 7th February, Zelensky filed a police report. During an appearance in Odessa, he had been tailed by various cars, and he also claimed to have been monitored in Kyiv. The Minister of the Interior, Arsen Avakov, announced that one of the drivers who had been arrested in connection with the matter showed a secret-service ID. In March, the SBU indeed confirmed that a wiretap had been installed near Studio Kvartal 95's offices. The agency also said that the investigation in question was unrelated to the presidential candidate, but refused to divulge any further information due to 'national security' concerns.

As the election campaign was gaining momentum, Zelensky kept conspicuously out of the spotlight. He skipped the television debates, and only gave interviews sporadically. When confronted with critical questions from journalists, Zelensky was quick to break character. On 18th January, a reporter from *Radio Svoboda* was waiting for him outside on the street. The radio station had done its research and discovered that Zelensky owned an offshore business in Cyprus with operations in Russia. While not illegal, such operations were certainly frowned upon in Ukraine. Zelensky refused to answer the questions, snapped at the reporter and hurried into his Land Rover. Later that same day, he apologised for his conduct. In a press release, he announced that the Cyprus-based business only existed in order to receive the broadcasting royalties payable by Russian companies, and that the money was properly channelled back to Ukraine.

On 21st January, Zelensky gave an interview to the reputable newspaper *Ukrainska Pravda*. He tried to charm the young reporter by making jokes, but when the journalist refused to budge, Zelensky had difficulty concealing his frustration.

Zelensky much preferred to campaign on stage. Even in the midst of the election battle, none of his regular performances were cancelled, and Kvartal 95 continued to tour the country. The group even performed free of charge for underprivileged Ukrainians. Zelensky's team gave shows at the exhausting rate of two per day, featuring Olena Kravets as the officious Yulia Tymoshenko and Yuriy Krapov as a dopey Petro Poroshenko, fretting over how he might stay on as President. Some time later, the 'Honesty' anti-corruption agency would rule that from the second half of 2018 onwards, episodes of *Vecherniy Kvartal* contained political advertising.

In the final show before the election, Zelensky addressed the topic personally – delivering a serious message with a playful wink. 'Earlier this evening, I said that we would not participate in propaganda,' Zelensky said at the end of the show. Then, grinning: 'And we kept our word, did we not? It wouldn't have helped anyway, because you can all make up your own minds. You all know what you need to do on the 31st [election day].'

Kvartal 95 then performed a song about Ukraine. It was a cover of a well-known pop song – by then the classic way to end every episode. For the finale, a choir of little girls in white dresses came on stage:

When you are no longer here
What kind of world will you leave behind?
One of freedom,
Or of smoke and fire?
For future generations
There is a universal law:
Do not live for yesterday.

Where will we ourselves be?
Will we sing our own song?
Will we see our children grow up,
Or our children's children?
Imagine the country the way you would like it to be,
One to live in and be proud of!

The song was kitsch and cliché, but hit its mark – Zelensky and his colleagues seemed to truly believe it, and tears flowed in the auditorium.

Traditionally no campaigning is allowed on the eve of an election in Ukraine. But on 30th March 2019 1+1 broadcast Kvartal 95 shows all day, with the exception of a documentary about Ronald Reagan – the actor who became the 40th President of the United States, and put an end to the Cold War. The American film was dubbed in Ukrainian, with Reagan's voice supplied by Zelensky.

Polling day: *Zelensky votes in the Presidential Election.*
IMAGO/ITAR-Tass

On election day on 31st March, Zelensky won a clear victory over Poroshenko (30.2 per cent vs 15.95 per cent). But because no candidate achieved an outright majority, a second election was scheduled for 21st April. On that day, a comedian and a billionaire with over 20 years' political experience would battle it out for the presidency.

The established order was already rocked to its foundations, however. Even before the day of the first election was out, Tymoshenko made allegations of 'mendacious' exit polls, voter fraud, and 'provocations.' Poroshenko, seated far from Zelensky, kept a stiff upper lip. 'Tomorrow is the first of April,' he said in one response. 'Starting from the second, the time for jokes is over.'

In an effort to turn the tide, Poroshenko pulled out all the stops. Poroshenko's 5 Kanal and TV station Pryamyi Kanal (owned by a Poroshenko supporter) launched an all-out smear campaign against Zelensky, painting the actor as a junkie with no political experience, and who was bent on selling Ukraine out to the Russians. Because Zelensky was merely Kolomoyskyi's puppet – according to the reports – he planned to give the nationalised PrivatBank straight back to the oligarch, sending the Ukrainian national budget into yet another tailspin.

Enormous roadside billboards showed Poroshenko and Putin posed as fighting cocks, facing one another. The message? A vote for Zelensky was a vote for Russia.

For weeks, Poroshenko had been challenging Zelensky to a televised election debate, but to no avail. In a television studio, Zelensky might start to resemble an ordinary politician. When the pressure became too great and Zelensky faced accusations of hiding in the shadows, he changed tack and went on the offensive. Ukraine's greatest performer announced that he was prepared to debate Poroshenko in Kyiv's 70,000-seat Olympic Stadium on 19th April. To augment the athletic nature of the encounter, Zelensky proposed that both candidates first undergo a doping test – in direct reference to Poroshenko's allegations of Zelensky's supposed drug use. And so the Ukrainian TV viewers were treated to scenes of both candidates giving blood: Poroshenko in the stadium, and Zelensky in a private clinic. Both candidates tested negative.

Poroshenko believed he would have the advantage, since the language for the 'debate of the century' would be Ukrainian. And indeed, Zelensky's crew was worried. His political adviser, Andriy Bohdan, who hailed from western Ukraine, had already decided in November that from then on, nobody was to speak Russian to Zelensky. 'I made myself very unpopular with his friends,' Bohdan recalled. 'Everyone hated me. But I forced them to speak Ukrainian to him.'

When the big day came, tens of millions of people sat glued to their TVs, and not only in Ukraine. The debate was followed with keen interest by neighbouring countries. Russia – where public polling had been a mere formality for 20 years – even experienced some hype. Imagine: a real debate, held during genuine, fair, democratic elections!

Though the audience in the stadium was lower than expected, the viewers were not disappointed. Poroshenko made a presidential entrance with plenty of hand-waving and thumbs-upping. On the stage, he surrounded himself with Ukrainian war veterans in camo gear, some with crutches. They made a show of holding up blue-and-yellow Ukrainian flags, and threw Zelensky menacing looks. While his opponent was speaking, Poroshenko stood an intimidating one-and-a-half metres away. Next to the oligarch's hulking frame, it became evident just how small Zelensky was.

But Poroshenko struggled to take control of the debate. Despite all attempts at pathos, the incumbent President's voice was too forced and hasty, even shrill. Zelensky, by contrast, was a consummate master of timing and delivery. Moreover, his

Ukrainian was flawless, to Bohdan's great relief. 'Poroshenko thought he'd be able to trip Zelensky up on umming and aahing, and resorting to Russian. But Zelensky not only successfully defended himself, he also launched his own attacks, in Ukrainian.'

Zelensky had a few pieces of paper with him. Questions for Poroshenko, submitted by Ukrainian citizens online, he claimed. Others suspected he was using cheat-sheets.

'How can it be that Ukraine is one of the poorest countries in Europe, when it is governed by the richest President in history?' Zelensky asked. 'How do you sleep at night?'

In a bad temper, Poroshenko responded: 'If you knew in what condition I had inherited the country in 2014, with no treasury, no gold reserves and no army, you wouldn't even be asking that question. And at a time when you, I'm sorry to say, were insulting our nation with your jokes.'

Poroshenko broached the subject of Zelensky's lack of experience: 'You have said that you are eager to learn the art of the presidency.' Then, turning to the audience, he asked: 'Would you board an aeroplane if the pilot was still learning to fly? Would you undergo an operation just to give the surgeon a bit of practice?'

Both candidates accused each other of business dealings in Russia. Zelensky with his films and series, and Poroshenko with his Roshen sweets, which lined the shelves of every Russian supermarket. Poroshenko then played another ace, and brought up Zelensky's commercial ties with the infamous Ihor Kolomoyskyi.

Zelensky was unruffled: 'Let's talk about your business. I believe you privatised the Karl Marx factory at some point in the 90s, and turned it into the Roshen company?'

Andriy Bohdan was proved right: you win debates with preparation. For a full seven days, Zelensky had done nothing other than prepare for the face-off with Poroshenko.

Poroshenko then brought up the war, referring to Zelensky's TV speech from 1st March 2014, when he told Putin that he would be prepared to beg 'on his knees' if need be. 'One does not defend the nation by grovelling before Putin.'

But Zelensky was prepared for this, too. 'You have taken those words out of context. I am prepared to kneel for every mother whose son did not return from the front, for every child who has lost a father, for every wife who no longer has a husband.' Then, to Poroshenko: 'I invite you to do the same.'

Zelensky lowered himself to his knees, and Poroshenko had little choice but to follow suit.

After the debate, 50 per cent of Ukrainians felt that Zelensky had won, while 14 per cent thought Poroshenko was more convincing, according to opinion polls. Thirty per cent of those surveyed claimed to have a more negative opinion of Poroshenko after seeing the debate.

The only thing standing in the way of Zelensky's victory now was electoral fraud, which concerned Oleksiy Honcharuk, a young lawyer who occupied an important role in Zelensky's team. Zelensky's team had always focused on delivering a clear message, but the harsh reality of Ukrainian politics required more. They needed observers to monitor and ensure integrity at the polls, and lawyers to follow up on any allegations of voter fraud. Honcharuk knew that if the margin of victory were too narrow, Poroshenko could contest the result.

Honcharuk and Zelensky had already run through possible scenarios in the autumn of 2018. 'How do you intend to safeguard the result?' the young lawyer asked.

'We need to win with such a landslide that it won't be necessary,' Zelensky answered.

Honcharuk laughed. 'Who do you think you are, the Brazilian football team or something?'

'Yes,' replied Zelensky.

6. The Turbo Regime

On a glorious morning in May 2019, Volodymyr Zelensky was inaugurated as the sixth President of Ukraine.

Zelensky walked to the ceremony from his apartment near the Government buildings in the centre of Kyiv. Before the Ukrainian parliament building on Constitution Square, an enthusiastic crowd thronged behind crowd-control barriers decked out in Ukrainian blue-and-yellow. Zelensky was beaming, throwing out V-signs and high-fives to the audience. His Kvartal colleagues Mika Falatov and Yuriy Tkach, who were waiting behind the barriers, each received a polite kiss on the cheek. For the immensely tall Yevhen Koshovy, Zelensky leapt high into the air and planted a smacker on his shiny skull.

Inside, in the plenary hall of the Verkhovna Rada, the mood was less festive. The ministers and Prime Minister Volodymyr Hroysman, with party leader Arseniy Yatsenyuk at his side, wore bitter expressions. The newly retired Petro Poroshenko received thunderous applause from the members of his party – a rather inappropriate gesture during the new President's inauguration.

On 21st April, Zelensky had won round two of the presidential elections with an overwhelming majority of 73.2 per cent – over 13.5 million Ukrainians had voted for the former comedian and actor. Zelensky wanted to hit the ground running. Even during the election campaign, he had announced his desire to call new parliamentary elections as soon as possible. His party, Servant of the People, had had such high approval ratings, he was determined to secure an absolute majority.

To prevent Zelensky holding an early election to the Rada while he was still riding high in the polls, the sitting parties tried to postpone his inauguration until after 27th May. It was not until three weeks after the election results were announced that the Rada finally set a date for the ceremony: Monday 20th May, a work day that would prevent many of Zelensky's supporters from attending.

Delaying the inauguration was not the only trick up the Rada's sleeve. On 17th May, Yatsenyuk's party, the People's Front, suddenly announced its withdrawal from the governing coalition. According to Yatsenyuk, this meant the Rada then had 30 days in which form a new coalition, during which time Parliament could not be dissolved. In response, Zelensky stated that the People's Front and the Petro Poroshenko Bloc (now known as 'European Solidarity') had not held a majority in Parliament since 2016, meaning that constitutionally a coalition had not existed for years. One the eve of his inauguration, Zelensky shared an online video. 'The Rada is giving us grief,' he said with a sly grin. 'But two can play at that game.'

Presidential inaugurations in Ukraine are prone to mishaps. When Yanukovych tried to enter the Rada in 2010, the doors inadvertently shut in his face. At Poroshenko's 2014 inauguration, one of the honour guards dropped his rifle on the red carpet.

But Zelensky had rehearsed thoroughly beforehand. He energetically bounded up the parliamentary steps, then marched through the plenary hall up to the rostrum. After taking the presidential oath, he received the venerated symbols of his power: the presidential seal, his chain of office, and the gilded bulava, a replica of the historic mace that had served as the symbol of Ukrainian leadership since the reign of Cossack leader Bohdan Khmelnytsky (ca. 1595-1657). When the choir began their solemn hymn, Zelensky's eyes welled up and he gulped back tears. The First Lady looked on nervously.

Zelensky's inaugural speech was a declaration of war on the Rada and the established political class. In it, the new head of state made reference to Ronald Reagan: 'Allow me to cite the words of an American actor who became a marvellous President: The Government cannot solve our problems, the Government is our problem.'

He went on: 'I do not understand our current Cabinet, which shrugs its shoulders and says there is nothing they can do. Not true. There is something you can do. You can pick up a pen and paper, and free up your seat for those who think not merely about the next election, but about the generations to come. Write your letter of resignation. People will thank you for it.'

Outside on the street, where the ceremony was being broadcast on a large screen, there were shouts of joy. Inside, there were only sporadic claps of approval.

'Such tepid applause,' said Zelensky. 'Perhaps some are disgruntled at what I'm saying? Pity, since it is not me who is saying these things, but the people of Ukraine.'

A grim smirk appeared on Prime Minister Hroysman's face, simultaneously condescending and threatening, as if to say: try it if you dare. Zelensky continued straight on: 'I hereby dissolve the Verkhovna Rada. Long live Ukraine!'

The parliamentary elections were scheduled for 21nd July. But although Zelensky's Servant of the People had been registered since late 2017, it did not have a party structure. The first 'party congress' in January 2019 was an informal get-together with hamburgers and pizza.

And since his election, Zelensky had done virtually nothing to recruit new administrative staff. Still, on 13th July, Servant of the People presented a list of candidates, consisting primarily of external experts, social activists, small and medium-sized business owners, and acquaintances from Kvartal 95. Zelensky hoped that his party would grow into a leading reform movement in Ukraine. He would later say: 'I went in search of young people who were still true.'

The parliamentary elections surpassed Zelensky's wildest dreams. Servant of the People won 254 of the 424 seats (26 seats were not available, due to the Russian occupation of Crimea and the 'People's Republics' of Donetsk and Luhansk). The landslide victory meant that Zelensky had no need to form a coalition with Yatsenyuk or Poroshenko, but could instead appoint a Cabinet as he saw fit. Because the Ukrainian Parliament has only one chamber, the new President was automatically assured of enough support to pass the legislation he planned to reform the country with in the coming five years.

Within months of announcing his candidacy, Zelensky had turned Ukrainian politics upside-down. But a stunning victory was no guarantee of success. Zelensky's MPs were not all political heavyweights. In the province of Zaporizhia, for example, a wedding photographer, Serhiy Shtepa, won the seat. Oleksander Skichko – a 28-year-old media personality who had presented the Eurovision Song Festival in 2017 – won the seat in the Cherkasy 'oblast.' 'We just put "Team Zelensky" stickers on someone, and we had a winning candidate,' recalled Andriy Bohdan, Zelensky's political adviser. In more questionable cases, the new parliamentarians were vulgar fortune-seekers who showed little loyalty to the party. The candidates were also difficult to assemble under a single political banner. According to Bohdan, it was an 'ideological hodgepodge.'

In November 2019, the leaders of Servant of the People admitted to some internal confusion as to its politics. 'Our general outlook is libertarian,' said party chair Oleksander Kornienko, 'but the liberalist principles are not yet supported by all, so for the time being we must find a middle ground between liberal and socialist ideas.'

On 29th August, Zelensky presented the new Cabinet. It was a team of young technocrats, many of whom had enjoyed a prestigious education in western Europe or the United States. Hanna Novosad, aged only 29, was appointed Education Minister. Aged 34, the Minister of Social Affairs, Yulia Sokolovska, had already completed a training programme at the IMF. The odd-one-out was Arsen Avakov, an old hand who had been the Minister of the Interior since 2014. Zelensky also appointed his Prime Minster: Oleksiy Honcharuk, the young lawyer who advised his presidential election campaign. At 35, Honcharuk was the youngest Prime Minister in Ukrainian history.

Zelensky's ministerial team was youthful, good looking, ambitious – and spectacularly inexperienced. Within a very short time, the media started referring to them as the *Sorosyata* (the 'Soros-youngsters'), after George Soros, the American-Hungarian investor who had donated billions of dollars to promote liberal democracy in eastern Europe and the former Soviet Union.

New President: *Now Zelensky had to govern.*
Ukrainian Government

At the end of the summer, Zelensky released a documentary on the first 100 days of his presidency. He was interrogated by Stanislav Boklan, the actor who played the Prime Minister in *Servant of the People*. Zelensky still avoided real press interviews as much as possible and press conferences by his spokespeople were a rarity. He preferred to communicate with voters directly via social media and kept a close eye on the responses.

'It's time you showed some balls,' said someone by the name of Yuriy Krupp on Facebook in June 2019.

'Check your DMs,' Zelensky replied.

Andriy Bohdan, Zelensky's adviser, revealed that the new president sometimes texted him at 2am 'because some bot or other with 20 likes had said something mean about him. He's very sensitive to that kind of thing.' Bohdan was surprised because Zelensky had 'spent his entire career criticising other politicians.'

In September, Zelensky inadvertently featured in a scandal that would form the basis for the impeachment trial of Donald Trump.

The American president was searching for dirt on Joe Biden, former vice-president and his Democrat opponent in the upcoming presidential elections. The Trump team thought they had uncovered something useful in Ukraine.

Back in 2016, Biden had put major pressure on the Poroshenko Government to dismiss the then Ukrainian Prosecutor General Viktor Shokin. According to Washington and the EU, Shokin was an impediment to anti-corruption measures in Ukraine. Trump supporters, however, believed that the real reason was a (dormant) corruption inquiry into oligarch Mykola Zlochevsky, owner of the Burisma gas corporation, where Joe Biden's son, Hunter, had been a board member since 2014. Trump put two and two together and theorised that Biden senior had dismissed Shokin in order to protect his Hunter from prosecution.

On 25th July, president Trump called Zelensky and asked him for 'a favour.'

'There's a lot of talk about Biden's son, that Biden stopped the prosecution,' said Trump, 'and a lot of people want to find out about that, so whatever you can do with the Attorney General would be great.'

According to the playbook, Zelensky should have answered: 'President Trump, the Ukrainian Public Prosecutor's Office is an independent body, I cannot tell them what to do.'

Instead, he played up to the American president: '[...] the next Prosecutor General will be 100 per cent my person, my candidate,' Zelensky assured him. 'He or she will look into the situation, specifically to the company that you mentioned in this issue.'

Zelensky was under a lot of pressure. The United States was a crucial ally and Trump knew it. One week before the telephone conversation, the American president had suspended a delivery of US$400 million weapons to Ukraine. Immediately following the conversation, the Zelensky Government was inundated with requests from the Trump administration, first from Trump's lawyer Rudi Giuliani, and then from White House members of staff.

Zelensky actually had no intention of dancing to Trump's tune. Andriy Yermak, a lawyer and producer appointed by Zelensky as Presidential Aide for Foreign Policy Issues, listened politely to Giuliani, but did as little as possible.

On 18th September, the *Washington Post* wrote that a whistleblower had wiretapped the conversation and reported Trump for potential abuse of power. In late September, the $400 million worth of military aid was released. The Ukrainian President agreed the White House could publish a transcript of his call with Trump. Zelensky did not expect it to include his side of the conversation, but it did. Zelensky came across as a spineless Washington puppet. He was furious.

In reality, Zelensky was charting his own course – whether his Western friends liked it or not. On 7th September, at Boryspil airport in Kyiv, the Ukrainian president welcomed 35 Ukrainians who had been arrested by Russia some time before. Most were sailors who had been imprisoned during the Kerch Strait Incident on 25th November 2018. The Russians, for their part, also released several prominent Ukrainian activists, including a filmmaker, Oleh Sentsov, who had previously been sentenced to 20 years' imprisonment for 'terrorism' in Crimea – a politically motivated verdict.

In exchange for the release of the Ukrainians, Kyiv set free a number of convicted separatists. To secure the deal, Zelensky and Russia's President Putin spoke directly to each other on the phone.

Zelensky considered the prisoner exchange a triumph. 'This is the first step in ending the war,' he told the press. But the President had gone to great lengths to achieve his goal. Five former officers from the Berkut riot police, suspected of firing at demonstrators during the Maidan uprising, were freed. And they were not the only ones.

No sooner had Sentsov embraced his daughter at the airport in Kyiv, than a Ukrainian separatist commander, Volodymyr Tsemakh, boarded a plane for Moscow – to the great frustration of the Dutch Government.

Tsemakh was an important witness in the investigation into the 2014 downing of flight MH17, whose victims included 196 Dutch citizens. Several months prior, the international

Joint Investigation Team leading the inquiry into the crash had announced its intention to prosecute three Russians Igor Girkin, Sergey Dubinsky and Oleg Pulatov, and a Ukrainian, Leonid Kharchenko. Less than a week later, agents from the Ukrainian secret service kidnapped Volodymyr Tsemakh during an operation deep in rebel territory. This spectacular operation resulted in the death of one Ukrainian soldier, and injury to another.

Despite serious suspicions of terrorism and protests by the Ukrainian prosecutor Oleh Peresada, the court in Kyiv decided to lift the remand on Tsemakh on 5th August. All evidence points to the judge having done so at the behest of the Ukrainian President. Zelensky was unaffected by the Dutch frustrations. 'They know why I made that decision,' the President told the Ukrainian press a month later. 'They know that Ukrainian citizens are my top priority.'

Zelensky had more on his plate than just flight MH17. The Ukrainian President was working hard to resolve the stalled peace process in eastern Ukraine.

In 2015, the Minsk II Agreement had set out the conditions for peace: the withdrawal of troops, returning control of the border with Russia to Ukraine, local elections, and an autonomous status for the regions under separatist control in Donetsk and Luhansk.

But Ukraine had signed Minsk II with a knife at its throat. For many Ukrainians, the concessions made at the time by

President Poroshenko were unacceptable. And yet in 2018, Poroshenko still succeeded in getting a bill through the Rada granting 'special status' to Donetsk and Luhansk that would come into force as soon as the remaining steps in the peace process had been taken. The Minsk agreements, however, were unclear about the order of these measures. According to Russia, the autonomous status would be declared first, followed by local elections. Only then would control of the border be handed over to Ukraine.

In Kyiv's eyes, this was a nightmare. As long as pro-Russian troops held control of Donetsk and Luhansk, normal elections were an impossibility and would allow the same 'leaders' as before – puppets of Moscow – to take power. And with control of two autonomous regions within Ukraine's borders, Putin would retain considerable influence in Ukrainian politics, and Kyiv could forget about its hopes of EU or NATO membership. Little wonder that the negotiations on the implementation of Minsk II had been deadlocked for years.

In an attempt to resolve the sensitivities surrounding the elections, the then German minister for Foreign Affairs, Frank-Walter Steinmeier, thought up an intricate compromise. The regions' autonomy would come into force temporarily following the closure of the polls at 8pm on polling day and the 'special status' would become permanent as soon as independent observers from the Organization for Security and Co-operation in Europe could confirm that the elections had been fair. It was a superficial solution that did not address the real underlying problem: that Russia was not interested in a sustainable solution for the Donbas, but wished to destabilise Ukraine.

Nevertheless, on 1st October Zelensky put his name to the Steinmeier agreement, which led to furious protests on the streets of Kyiv and cries of 'No to capitulation!' by demonstrators.

Zelensky thought he could explain everything away. On 10th October he held his first major press conference before the Ukrainian media. On this occasion, too, Zelensky and his advisers planned something out-of-the-ordinary. President Putin and the Belarusian leader, Alexander Lukashenko, were well-known for their interminable press conferences, but the Ukrainian President set a world record of 14 hours – and received a certificate afterwards on behalf of the *Guinness Book of Records*. The plan to host the event in a McDonald's restaurant had met with some objection in Washington, and so Zelensky opted for a trendy food court in the centre of Kyiv. The President sat at a wooden table, and was joined by rotating groups of journalists – Zelensky wanted to be able to 'look everyone in the eye.' Fancy hamburgers were served to the participants.

'My primary goal is to end the war,' said Zelensky. 'How will we do it? We'll talk about that in a minute.' Less than five minutes later, he reiterated one of the necessary preconditions that had so plagued the Minsk process: 'Local elections in the Donbas will only be possible once all troops have withdrawn.'

Talks with Russia: *Zelensky with Germany's Chancellor Angela Merkel, French President Emmanuel Macron, and Russia's President Vladimir Putin, in Paris, 2019.*
IMAGO/ITAR-TASS

On 9th December 2019, Zelensky travelled to Paris for negotiations between Ukraine, Russia, France and Germany. On 6th June 2014, the 70th anniversary of D-Day in France, the leaders of these countries had come together for the first time, but nothing had been achieved in the five years since, other than a ceasefire that was violated almost daily. More than 14,000 soldiers and civilians had lost their lives since the start of the conflict. Zelensky was optimistic, and made a V-sign with his fingers upon entering the Elysée. The French President, Emmanuel Macron, also appeared hopeful. Putin was expressionless, as always, and the German Chancellor Angela Merkel exuded little confidence in a positive resolution.

France and Germany saw the meeting as a new beginning. Putin and Zelensky were meeting face to face for the first time. Macron said: 'We see this as a long-term investment.'

The four parties sat down at the negotiating table at 6.30pm. At around 9pm, Macron and Merkel retired, leaving the Ukrainians and the Russians with each other. The two European leaders had stressed the need for Putin to make concessions – Zelensky had already done so. But though civil, the Russian president refused to budge: only once all the conditions of Minsk II had been fulfilled would control of the border be returned to Ukraine. The parties attempted to resolve other matters, such as the withdrawal of troops from flashpoints on the front. But here, too, the negotiations were deadlocked. The Ukrainian minister for the Interior, Arsen Avakov, recalled how Putin's adviser Vladislav Surkov, who was responsible for the Kremlin's Ukraine policy, slammed his papers down on the table and said: 'That is not what we agreed on!'

Zelensky, too, became more and more agitated. On the other side of the table, Moscow's politicians were claiming to speak on behalf of the 'residents of the Donbas' – his people. According to Avakov, the Ukrainian president let fly at Russia's Foreign Affairs minister, Sergey Lavrov. 'How can you sit there and nod your head like that?' Zelensky asked, irritated: 'I know all those villages and towns, I have crossed them on foot, all the way to the border. You, Mr Lavrov, have not!'

The negotiations in Paris did not produce any concrete results. At the ensuing press conference held after midnight, Macron said that Putin and Zelensky would meet again in four months' time. Zelensky confirmed that he would be amenable, but Putin had other ideas. Despite many invitations from Zelensky, the two men would never meet again.

Zelensky was making spectacular progress on domestic policy. Under the leadership of the 35-year-old lawyer Honcharuk, the government passed one bill after another, and all were rushed through at breakneck speed by Zelensky's absolute majority in the Rada.

And just as well. In 2019, Ukraine was still the poorest country in Europe, with an average per capita income of US$300 per month. The World Economic Forum's Global Competitiveness Rating ranked Ukraine 85th in the world. Transparency International rated Ukraine 126th for corruption, and put the independence of the courts at 105 – lower than Russia.

The Honcharuk Government refused to be intimidated. The Cabinet made short work of problematic legislation on construction, real-estate, customs and mobile telephony. Honcharuk pruned the privileges of Naftohaz, the all-powerful oil and gas company. The administration embarked on a thorough reform of the Government, making it significantly easier to dismiss public servants. The baby was occasionally thrown out with the bathwater. Because the Honcharuk

Government planned to clean house in the public prosecutor's office, 1339 officials from the Heneralna Prokuratura were forced to reapply for their own jobs, and not everybody passed the rigorous, 6,000-question re-entrance exam. Others were dismissed due to anonymous allegations of 'personal enrichment.' The mass dismissals at the Heneralna Prokuratura caused an enormous backlog of cases.

In the spring of 2020, the engine of the Honcharuk Government's 'turbo regime' began to sputter. In September 2019, the head of the National Security and Defence Council, Oleksander Danylyuk, resigned. 'Zelensky has started listening to people who play up to him,' he said.

Andriy Bohdan, the key adviser who made Zelensky President, was sacked in February 2020. Although rumours had been circulating for some time about Bohdan's aggressive treatment of colleagues and journalists, the exact reason for his dismissal was not clear. Zelensky called him an 'unwelcome spouse,' Bohdan recalled: 'He said: "I don't know exactly what you are doing right or wrong, but I do know that you are annoying the hell out of me."'

In March 2020, the entire Honcharuk Cabinet fell apart. In January, an anonymous YouTube channel published recordings of a meeting between Prime Minister Honcharuk, the Finance minister Oksana Markarova, and several top officials including the acting director of the National Bank, in which Honcharuk spoke disparagingly of his President. According to Honcharuk,

Zelensky erroneously correlated the recent rise of Ukraine's currency, the hryvnia, and the emergence of a budget deficit: how can we have less money if the hryvnia is worth more now?

'Zelensky has a very primitive grasp of economic processes,' said Honcharuk on the recording. 'You need to explain it to him using a story... Listen Vova, the fact that the dollar has dropped means that after New Year, the potato salad...'

'...won't cost more than it did the previous year,' someone else interjected.

Honcharuk admitted being audible on the unauthorised recording, but claimed it had been edited. The Prime Minister offered his resignation. Initially Zelensky wished to hear nothing of it, but in early March during an extraordinary session of the Rada, he announced that Honcharuk's Government would be stepping down.

Zelensky tried to justify the move. 'Although this is the first Government that is not corrupt, refraining from stealing is not enough,' he said: 'This is a Government with new faces, but we also need new brains and hearts. This Government knows what to do, but the knowledge alone is not sufficient, we also need to work, work, work.'

The new Government came under the leadership of Denys Shmyhal, the 45-year-old former Regional Development Minister. Of the 15 ministers from the first Cabinet, only five remained.

According to Ukrainian media, the secret service, the SBU, told Zelensky who had made the unauthorised recording of Honcharuk, but no legal proceedings were set in motion. The case was declared a matter of national security, and the investigation disappeared into a drawer.

In March, the Prosecutor General, Ruslan Riaboshapka, was suddenly shown the door. Zelensky had called Riaboshapka '100 per cent my man' in his conversation with Trump, but he lasted only six months. According to the dismissed head of the Public Prosecutor's Office, the Ukrainian President no longer felt assured of Riaboshapka's 'complete loyalty.'

Zelensky wanted results: criminal proceedings and convictions. 'He named names, and talked about the need to start cases against them, to convict them of crimes,' said Riaboshapka of his meetings with the President. The Prosecutor General tried to explain that due process was important. Riaboshapka refused to bring a case against Petro Poroshenko, for example. 'What they put on my desk was just legal garbage,' the dismissed Prosecutor General later said. 'There was no evidence whatsoever.'

'If you're not getting results, then you shouldn't be there,' were Zelensky's own words on Riaboshapka's dismissal. The new Prosecutor General was Iryna Venediktova, who was involved in the inquiry into Poroshenko as head of the federal police. 'I have no doubts about her yet,' said Zelensky. And she proceeded apace. In July, Poroshenko announced that he had been charged with 24 cases. In September, his lawyers said that the number had grown to 58.

Zelensky believed that he was doing what he promised: rooting out corruption. But the West was furrowing its brow over the prosecution of Ukraine's former president. 'I find it imprudent,' said Lithuanian Foreign Affairs Minister Linas Linkevičius: 'Ukraine will start to resemble countries where the solution to the opposition is to throw them in jail.'

The dismissals continued unabated. In April, the heads of the tax and customs authorities were removed from office, and Ukraine's National Anti-Corruption Agency, the NABU, launched an investigation against them, despite the fact that the two heads in question were well-known anti-corruption figures. In June, the head of the National Bank, Yakiv Smoliy, tendered his resignation, claiming to have done so at Zelensky's suggestion.

Zelensky started complaining of 'administrative anaemia,' and that it was impossible to find good people. 'Whenever we appoint a new minister for Education or Culture, the very next day the media reports that they're already in Akhmetov or Kolomoyskyi's pockets.' According to Melinda Haring, deputy director of the Atlantic Council's Eurasia Center, the President himself was the cause of the problem. Zelensky's reformers had often left well-paid jobs in the private sector to work for him, Haring said. And as gratitude, not only were they out on the street from one day to the next, but they were prosecuted besides. 'If I were in the Zelensky Government,' Haring said, 'I would think twice before bringing court cases against people who had done many good things.'

The exodus of good administrators slowly eroded the foundations of Zelensky's reform agenda. According to research by the Ukraine press agency *RBK-Ukraina*, in late 2020 the President had the confidence of roughly half of the MPs representing Servant of the People. The other half, wrote the agency, were working in the interests of 'other stakeholders.' This is less strange than it might seem, because MP salaries were low. The President of the Rada only earned around US$1400 per month after tax.

Buying parliamentary influence was a simple matter. Journalists at *Bihus.info* analysed the voting behaviour of the Rada members, and came to the conclusion that of the 426 parliamentarians, 70 represented the interests of the powerful oligarch Ihor Kolomoyskyi, and 100 were in the pocket of the similarly influential Rinat Akhmetov. *RBK-Ukraina* reported that Kolomoyskyi had around 20-30 representatives from Servant of the People on his payroll. If the need arose, Kolomoyskyi could mobilise 40 members. The MPs all denied any involvement with Kolomoyskyi.

In the spring of 2020, Zelensky brought a proposal before the Verkhovna Rada to reform the banking system, which was intended to make it impossible for the PrivatBank nationalised by Poroshenko ever to return to Kolomoyskyi. To slow things down, a group of 28 parliamentarians – including members of Servant of the People – submitted a whopping 16,000 amendments to the bill. Ultimately only 200 of Zelensky's 254 members voted in favour of the proposal. The 'Anti-Kolomoyskyi Bill' could only be passed with the support of Poroshenko's European Solidarity party and right-wing liberals from The Voice.

Under these circumstances Ukraine was hit by the Covid-19 pandemic. Around 3-5 million Ukrainians were employed as seasonal workers abroad. With the borders closed, these millions of citizens were left without income. In the second half of 2020, the economy shrank by nearly 10 per cent.

The population panicked. When travelling Ukrainians were evacuated and quarantined in the region of Poltava, protests broke out. Buses full of returned travellers were pelted with stones. The police only got the situation under control with the help of the national guard.

Because the Cabinet had been disbanded in March, a new Minister for Health was left to combat the fast-spreading epidemic. When Ilya Yemets let slip in the Rada that the new virus was 'killing all the pensioners,' he was summarily replaced.

To nip the growing unrest in the bud, Zelensky proposed to his ministers that he deliberately infect himself with Covid-19, and go into isolation in the presidential palace. 'So that people understand it's not the black death,' he later said, 'and so that we don't all sink into depression.'

His ministers advised against the idea. In June, Olena Zelenska tested positive for Covid-19, and Zelensky himself contracted the virus in November. As a precautionary measure, he spent his corona-time in the hospital.

As the second Covid wave hit Europe, Zelensky – despite the ubiquitous travel restrictions – left for Brussels. The EU summit was too important to miss. He was greeted with an extended elbow by a masked President of the European Council, Charles Michel, while the EU President, Ursula von der Leyen, went into isolation when a member of staff fell ill.

The stakes were high. In 2014, the EU and Ukraine had signed an association agreement establishing economic ties. The agreement allowed Ukrainians to travel to Schengen countries without a visa, which – aside from the practical advantages for Kyiv – carried great symbolic value. Both Brussels and Kyiv showed interest in developing their relationship.

But Brussels was sceptical. 'According to many observers, the pace of reforms has slowed down recently, including on the implementation of the Association Agreement commitments,' blogged EU foreign affairs representative Josep Borrell shortly before the summit. Anti-corruption measures were a particular source of concern. Ukraine's National Anti-Corruption Bureau (NABU) was under Government control; reforms in the judicial system were sluggish, and Brussels was worried about the resignation of the anti-corruption specialist and prosecutor Nazar Kholodnytsky. In Brussels, there was some doubt as to whether Zelensky even wanted reform.

Zelensky knew of the EU's gripes. Rumours in Ukraine suggested that Brussels wanted to impose restrictions on the no-visa policy once the borders reopened after the pandemic. To improve the tone, the Ukrainian president brought a gift for Von der Leyen's deputy. The Order of Prince Yaroslav the Wise (978-1054) was ceremoniously bestowed upon Vice-President Maroš Šefčovič, as a token of gratitude for his role in 'strengthening Ukraine's international reputation.' The EU treated President Zelensky with kid gloves. In Brussels, they knew that the presidential administration in Kyiv was sensitive to criticism. 'Even if I carefully started out with something like: "We are your friends and wish to help, and so..." they got defensive straight away,' a Western diplomat told the Ukrainian paper *Yevropeiska Pravda*. To Zelensky, open criticism was completely out of the question. The President was well aware of the negative impact on his country's image whenever Western leaders called Ukraine 'corrupt.'

Brussels proceeded with caution. After the summit, the EU announced that the integration of Ukraine would continue, starting with an Open Skies agreement integrating Ukrainian and EU airspace. Zelensky was very pleased. 'It was a really great summit,' he wrote on Facebook. 'Because we are of interest. Promising. We are confident, and on the way to fully-fledged EU membership.'

The reality was more complicated, as Zelensky himself knew only too well. In the summer of 2020, journalists were permitted to shadow and interview him on the back seat of his car.

'You've been leading the country for a year now,' said one journalist, as the presidential escort trundled over Ukraine's abominable roads. 'What stands out to you most?'

'That we don't realise just what kind of condition we're in,' Zelensky replied. With emotion, he said: 'We work, we pay our taxes, we go on holiday, but if you take a closer look, you realise that everything is in shambles.'

'So in plain Ukrainian: it's one big shitheap?'

'Exactly,' Zelensky nodded. 'A complete shitheap!'

Zelensky had been disabused of many illusions since the start of his presidency. He had promised that he would leave the presidential palace on Bankova street with its gold leaf and kitsch bronze statues and move into modern offices. But because of the associated cost (tens of millions of US$), the plan was abandoned.

During his election campaign, he had said that the Government employees' country residences would be repurposed to house orphaned children. But due to security concerns, he and his family had already moved into the ostentatious presidential 'chalet' on the outskirts of Kyiv.

During his inaugural speech in the Verkhovna Rada, he had ordained that no portraits of him should be hung up in public spaces. 'I'd rather you hung up photos of your own children,' he said, 'and look them in the eyes before you make any decisions.' In the meantime, he had realised that there was also a sacred aspect to the office, and that the president needs to be more than just a cool guy.

Zelensky had also realised that he would be unable to fulfil his promise to put things right within a single presidential term. 'I promised a whole list of reforms, but now that I'm at work, the list is getting longer and longer,' Zelensky concluded in spring 2020. 'I therefore say: to get through the entire list, one presidential term is not enough.'

7. Confrontation

If Oleksander Novikov had been sitting down, he would have fallen off his chair. On 28th October 2020, the head of the National Agency on Corruption Prevention (NACP) spread out the pages of a decree by the Constitutional Court of Ukraine across the conference table. The paper was still warm from the laser printer.

The *Ukrainska Pravda* was filming Novikov for a documentary, when a panicked staffer rushed in unexpectedly with important news.

'I've never seen anything like this,' said Novikov as he perused the document with increasing surprise. Laying the decree beside an open legal code, the director giggled nervously as he scanned the relevant passages with his index finger: 'This puts a bomb beneath our anti-corruption activities, do you understand?'

As Ukraine's highest court of law, the Constitutional Court interprets the constitution in terms of laws and other legal acts. Although its 18 judges enjoy a high degree of independence, the Court has a bad reputation. In 2003, it granted president Kuchma (1994-2005) approval for an unconstitutional third term, which ultimately he did not use. Under his successor, Yanukovych (2010-2014), the Court undid the political changes put in place by the 2004 Orange Revolution. In early 2019, it scrapped the law against illegal 'personal enrichment,' instantly dismissing 65 open legal cases. Just like large portions of Ukraine's judiciary, the Constitutional Court has not been immune to shady dealings. To the contrary, some critics believe that Ukraine's most highly-placed judges underpin corruption.

With its latest move, however, the Constitutional Court had smacked Zelensky's anti-corruption campaign square in the jaw. Since 2016, all Ukrainian public servants had been required to declare all of their income and assets, such as property, savings, shares, and other commercial interests. Those who possessed more than they declared could be prosecuted under Article 366-1 of the Ukrainian Criminal Code. The Constitutional Court had declared that Article 366-1 was unconstitutional and that the public declaration register had to be discontinued. The legal justification for the decree was convoluted and incomprehensible, but Novikov from the NACP knew the consequences straight away. He said: 'This doesn't just take us back to 2013 – now we're right back in 1991.'

The Court had reached its decision following a complaint by representatives from two parties in the Verkhovna Rada: the pro-Russian Opposition Platform – For Life and For the Future, a party under the control of oligarch Ihor Kolomoyskyi. According to Ukrainian media, the top judges were also using the decree to whitewash their own activities. The Chairman, Oleksander Tupytsky, for example, had neglected to declare land that he purchased in Russian-occupied Crimea in 2018.

According to Andriy Yermak, who had become Zelensky's chief of staff, the decree had been paid for by corrupt politicians and businesspeople – an 'anti-presidential coalition of oppositional and oligarchic groups.' The very same day, the public register containing the declarations of four million Ukrainian public servants went offline.

President Zelensky had been forewarned of the imminent decree. His representative at the Court, Fedir Venislavsky, had called him the day before. Venislavsky said of the phone conversation: 'To say that the President was angry would be quite an understatement.'

The Court's decree triggered an acute crisis. With one fell swoop the Constitutional Court had ended the fight against corruption, which had serious consequences for the association agreement with the EU (which was already sceptical of Ukraine's progress) and put the financial and military assistance from the US on shaky ground. Anti-corruption was also a nonnegotiable precondition when applying for loans from the IMF and the World Bank – a financial lifeline for Ukraine.

Since the start of the war in 2014, international investments had evaporated and Covid had dented economic growth. 'This throws us right back into Russia's lap,' said an activist from the Anti-Corruption Action Centre, Vitaliy Shabunin. 'This is not just about corruption, but about the survival of the country as such.'

Zelensky felt the same. The day after the Constitutional Court's announcement, he called an emergency session of the National Security and Defence Council of Ukraine (NSDC), a body consisting of the chiefs of police, security services and armed forces along with the Prime Minister, parliamentary chair, the ministers, and the President. In the past, the security council had primarily fulfilled a coordinating role, but ever since the war its authorisations had been broadened to include the power to overrule.

During the meeting, a grim Zelensky summarised the consequences of the Court's decree: 'We will be deprived of all international financial and other support, and our developmental projects will be put on hold. The World Bank's aid will dry up. We'll have a huge hole in our budget. And the worst part is we don't know what the Constitutional Court has in store for us tomorrow, or the next day.'

The National Security and Defence Council ordered the anti-corruption agency NACP to reopen and continue monitoring of the declaration register immediately. The Security Council believed the action was justified as the Constitutional Court's decision was a 'threat to national security.' The next day, the register went back online.

That same day, Zelensky submitted a bill to the Verkhovna Rada, nullifying the Constitutional Court's decision and dismissing the judges involved. The measure was unconstitutional. According to the Ukrainian constitution, the Court's judges cannot be dismissed, they can only resign. The act was condemned by two authoritative bodies from the European Council, and in a harsh letter to Zelensky, the President of the Venice Commission on constitutional law and the Group of States against Corruption spoke out against 'a gross violation of the constitution and the principle of separation of powers.'

Many Ukrainians saw things differently. On the evening of 30th October, hundreds of protesters gathered before the building of the Constitutional Court, holding placards saying 'Send the traitor judges to Rostov' – the Russian city where Yanukovych fled after the Maidan uprising in 2014. Many demonstrators carried large photos of the refugee president. Zelensky fanned the flames with a furious Facebook post, mentioning a 'conspiracy against the president and the country, forged by oligarchs and members of the old elite.' He made a reference to the date: All Saints' Day and Hallowe'en, the day when the spirits of the underworld emerge to walk the Earth. 'On Hallowe'en, all the political demons reveal their true faces,' Zelensky wrote, 'and you know their names.'

But the Rada had no intention of passing Zelensky's bill – much to the President's chagrin. 'In five or 10 years' time, nobody will remember the representatives' claims of "unconstitutionality,"' he said in a television interview, 'but everybody will remember how we tried to reform the judiciary.'

It was futile. To avoid a defeat in the Rada, Zelensky announced that he would seek advice from the Venice Commission. The answer came in December. Although the Commission was certainly critical of the Constitutional Court's decision, it saw no way to allow for the short-term replacement of judges.

Zelensky refused to let it go. In late December, the Government announced that chief judge Oleksander Tupytsky was to be suspended for two months because the Public Prosecutor's Office suspected him of bribery and forgery. When Tupytsky tried to enter the Constitutional court building in the new year, he was halted by security guards. After the two months had elapsed, Zelensky's advisers came up with a new tactic. The President repealed the presidential decree (ukase) that originally appointed Tupytsky and his colleague Oleksander Kasminin, thus effecting the two judges' de facto dismissal. The repeal led to a chaotic legal battle, during which both judges challenged their dismissal, and the Public Prosecutor's Office brought legal action against Ukraine's most highly-placed judges.

To Zelensky, the constitutional crisis was the straw that broke the camel's back. On his election in 2019, he thought that he could convince Ukraine of the need for change. Now, he was forced to acknowledge the true extent of the resistance among the corrupt elite. 'I am sorry to say that I have wasted one-and-a-half years trying to get my point across by engaging in dialogue,' he said in summer 2021. 'I'm sick of having to negotiate time and time again.'

Zelensky resorted to the heaviest weapon in his presidential artillery. On 2nd February 2021, the National Security and Defence Council imposed 'sanctions' on the MP and media magnate Taras Kozak, prohibiting any further broadcasting by the three channels he owned – NewsOne, 112 Ukraina and ZIK. Kozak's assets were also frozen for five years.

Under Ukrainian law intended to target the separatists in Donetsk and Luhansk, such drastic measures were permissible in cases of 'terrorism' or its financing. Now, however, Zelensky was deploying this anti-terror law against Ukraine's own judiciary.

According to the SBU security service, there were signs that Kozak was involved in the coal trade in the Donbas, which had continued as usual, to the benefit of the separatists. But there was an underlying motivation. In the Rada, Kozak represented the pro-Russian Opposition Platform – For Life party by Viktor Medvedchuk, a multi-millionaire and good friend of Putin's. Kozak's channels broadcast content critical of Zelensky's Government and occasionally repeated Kremlin rhetoric. Many suspected that in reality, the stations actually belonged to Medvedchuk. According to Zelensky's adviser Mykhailo Podolyak, the TV channels 'were actively and sometimes publicly used to spread foreign propaganda in Ukraine.'

The Ukrainian response was overwhelmingly positive – even among the press, where many journalists had been discontented with the propaganda being shown on NewsOne and 112 Ukraina for some time. The American embassy in Kyiv supported the move. The EU gave a mixed response, saying that while Ukraine had the right to protect itself against disinformation, it should not threaten freedom of speech.

'I am grateful to the representatives of society for understanding and supporting the necessity of this decision by the National Security and Defence Council,' Zelensky wrote on Facebook. 'Open propaganda requires a swift and decisive social response.'

Not everybody was on Zelensky's side, however. The Parliamentary chair Dmytro Razumkov, a confidant of Zelensky and a member of his election staff, found the move inappropriate. 'Sanctions are an effective means if we cannot impose punishments via Ukrainian law,' he told the *Babel* news site. 'But in this case, all the necessary instruments were available. And silencing television channels is a nasty business in any case.'

On 13th February, Zelensky's adviser Mykhailo Podolyak announced a new swathe of sanctions, before the associated decisions were even official. 'We will have another important sitting next week,' Podolyak wrote on Facebook. 'Otherwise we will never succeed in draining this swamp.'

In his Facebook post, Podolyak did not beat about the bush. 'Why does the president prefer the NSDC instruments? It's quite simple: he's had enough of having to wait endlessly for resolutions by executive and legislative bodies.' According to Podolyak, effective government by the Rada had become impossible, because difficult resolutions were hamstrung by horse-trading among established interests. 'Society wants solutions,' said Podolyak. 'And the NSDC is a direct instrument of power meant to tackle complex situations – situations that have gone unresolved for years.'

His standpoint was radical. President Zelensky wanted to be able to make decisions that were exempt from parliamentary control. And not only that. As long as the corrupt judiciary thwarted reform, Zelensky wished to deploy the Security Council against all Ukrainian citizens he believed constituted a threat to national security, without any intervention by the judiciary. 'We are talking about a very broad spectrum,' said party chairman Oleksander Kornienko: 'From mafia bosses to white collar criminals.'

On 19th February, the National Security and Defence Council announced sanctions against Viktor Medvedchuk, his wife, and against the partner of Taras Kozak. The Security Council also nationalised the Ukrainian section of the Samara-Western Direction oil pipeline which, according to Ukrainian media, was owned by Medvedchuk. Five Russian citizens were added to the sanctions list.

The National Security and Defence Council, whose staff under Zelensky had jumped from 160 to 237, imposed sanctions on a Russian-Ukrainian sports clothing chain, as well as on 19 Ukrainian mining and oil companies. The NSDC also imposed a flight ban on private jets landing in Moscow. The Council nationalised the Motor Sich airline, imposed sanctions on Ukrainian military officers suspected of treason, and on Ukrainian citizens suspected of smuggling or organised crime. Around 150 public servants were relieved of their posts by the NDSC. By the end of 2021, the Zelensky Government had sanctioned 1162 citizens and 680 legal entities. Around 100 citizens ended up on the list by mistake, the National Security and Defence Council reported.

On 12th March 2021, Zelensky recorded an online video message. 'I do not need to tell you that recent resolutions by the National Security and Defence Council have elicited quite a range of responses – some positive, but there is also understandable indignation among those who have come across their own names in the Council's decisions. Let me explain what is going on in words that anyone can understand. Ukraine is defending itself – defending itself against those who for years have dealt the country blow after blow.'

Ukrainian human rights organisations were outraged. 'Sanctions against our own citizens should only be possible if they are living abroad, or hiding in occupied regions of Ukraine (Crimea and the Donbas) and the Government has no other viable means of calling them to account,' wrote various organisations in a joint appeal issued on 6th April. 'The president's measures are not sanctions in an international legal sense – they are a directive form of governance.'

Many politicians agreed. 'You cannot simply replace the work of the country's institutions,' said the Fatherland party's Olena Kondratiuk, the new acting chair of the Rada. 'The NSDC has effectively become the Public Prosecutor's Office, the National Anti-Corruption Agency, the tax authority, the judiciary, and the list goes on.'

As the year progressed, the National Security and Defence Council took more and more political decisions. The Council decided that intervention was necessary in the monopolised cable television market, that the intelligence services needed re-evaluation, and that aircraft construction should be stimulated. The Council decreed that President Zelensky's order to plant a billion trees within three years should be carried out, and that the number of Covid-19 vaccinations should rise to 350,000 per day. The National Security and Defence Council also determined that defence spending should be increased to 5.95 per cent of GDP. In July 2021, the NSDC decided to temporarily replace the board of the Ukrainian National Railways.

The Security Council often did nothing more than rubber stamp resolutions that had been prepared by the presidential staff. 'We saw many of the agenda items only right before the meeting started,' said parliamentary chair Razumkov. 'Some parts of the sanctions list weren't even on paper,' the Minister of the Interior Arsen Avakov recalled, indignant. 'Even I, a member of the National Security and Defence Council, didn't have access to the papers. I said to Danilov [the Council secretary]: "Oleksiy, the names being read out now aren't even in my dossier, what the hell is going on here?" "Forgot to copy them," he said.' In an interview at the end of the year, Avakov explained that it was one of his reasons for leaving. 'I wanted no part of it.'

Zelensky, by contrast, was happy when taking stock in October 2021. 'It was very important to have founded the National Security and Defence Council, it has proven extremely effective as an institution. The financial cliques, the oligarchs, and the traitors to the nation are afraid, they feel the pressure daily. And people appreciate it, society has faith.' Then, threateningly: 'If you are a traitor, we will put you in your place.'

Zelensky was a man on a mission. He wanted to transform Ukraine into a modern country with a digital economy and high standard of living. The Government tackled Ukraine's legendarily poor roads. In December 2021, 14,000km of asphalt was laid, covering 40 per cent of the country's arterial network. To encourage tourism and buff up Ukraine's image, historic buildings and museums were restored. Zelensky dreamt of a business district, Kyiv City, and of a special presidential university equipped to train up the 'managers of the future.' The leadership started working towards a 'paperless Government' and the digitisation of the courts system under the slogan 'the judiciary in your smartphone.'

Even more important, however, were Zelensky's land reforms. Thirty years after the fall of the Soviet Union, the sale of agricultural land was still prohibited. In 2021, the Rada consented to the gradual release of some farmland.

During a meeting in August with the new American President, Joe Biden, Zelensky presented a detailed plan in Washington outlining 80 major projects for the 'transformation of Ukraine' over the next 10 years. The cost was US$277 billion. Without considerable foreign investment, these kinds of future plans were castles in the sky. But investors were thin on the ground: Ukraine was corrupt through and through, and still at war. In 2021, foreign investment was estimated to be US$6.5 billion.

Confronted with his country's seemingly insurmountable problems, Zelensky brought to bear the cast-iron discipline for which he was known. The President was proud that he had not put on a single gram in weight and only permitted himself his favourite snack – chips – once or twice a year. He was still an avid gym-goer, although he had less and less time to walk Nora, his White Swiss Herder, or Petya, his black miniature Schnauzer. He found it genuinely regrettable. After all his negative experiences with politicians, he had come to like people less, and his dogs more. In moments of weakness, he would relapse into his nicotine addiction, vaping on an e-cigarette.

'He has changed a lot,' said his Kvartal colleague, Oleksander Pikalov. 'He talks to people differently, is more analytical, and is less prone to losing his temper.' Zelensky used to be a volcano capable of erupting at any moment. Now, he kept his feelings to himself and was sometimes closed off. 'He has become wiser, stronger,' said Pikalov. 'Somehow or other, he is continually working on self-improvement, as though in some kind of internal dialogue with himself.'

Kvartal 95 had pressed on without their leader. During the initial months of his presidency, Zelensky still took the time to read through the team's material. When his schedule became too hectic, he continued to keep an eye on the old troupe's performances. According to Kvartal member Yuriy Velyky (who took over the role of the president), Zelensky often spoke on the phone to his former colleague and best friend Yevhen Koshovy. 'I understand that you have to make jokes,' Zelensky once said, 'but they are cutting pretty close to the quick.'

The consensus in Ukraine was quite different. In general, people found that Kvartal 95's jokes had lost their edge, especially when it came to the President.

Olena Zelenska continued to write for Kvartal 95 as before. But her other job as First Lady sometimes shone through in her work, said Oleksander Pikalov. 'When we started making jokes about child benefits, for example, Lena piped up and said: "You know that's not how it is."'

'But Lena, it's comedy,' I said, to which she replied: Yes, but humour still needs to be true.'

Although Olena was firmly against Volodymyr's decision to enter politics, she stepped into the role of First Lady with verve. The President's wife donned stylish clothes by Ukrainian designers and did not limit her activities to traditional areas, such as school nutrition and orphans. Working with a group of experts, she released a diversity handbook with advice on how to interact with people from other ethnicities, with disabilities, or people from the LGBTQ+ community. By Ukraine's standards it was incredibly modern, not to mention hip.

The couple's daughter Sasha, born in 2003, was less happy. When she was little Zelensky had no time for her, and although their relationship had improved over the years, she was starting to dread going to university sandwiched between two bodyguards. 'My daughter really doesn't want me to go for a second term,' Zelensky said. 'But no matter how much I love her, it all depends on how much progress we make.'

The challenge before him was immense. The acute crisis surrounding the Constitutional Court was no isolated incident, but the symptom of a broader problem. '"Corruption" is an inadequate word to describe the condition of Ukraine,' wrote Thomas de Waal from the Carnegie Center in 2016. De Waal continued: 'The problem is not that a well-functioning state has been corrupted [...] rather, those corrupt practices have constituted the rules by which the state has been run.' Bribes allowed MPs to holiday in the Maldives, for the chief of police to drive a Mercedes, and for the Chief Justice to build a seaside retreat. In a society where doing honest business was difficult, nearly everybody's hands were dirty.

The oligarchs perched at the top of this corrupt pyramid. According to Forbes, the wealth of the 100 richest Ukrainians totalled US$44.5 billion in 2021 – almost a quarter of that year's GDP (US$195 billion). The oligarchs' business model clashed with the values of a modern liberal state with a market economy. They earned their money by charging exorbitant prices in a monopolised marketplace, by paying hardly any tax, or by whitewashing criminal funds through complex corporate structures. To maintain their modus operandi, their power reached deep into the Government, the Parliament, the judiciary and the Ukrainian media. Some oligarchs, for instance, owned several television channels.

In the summer of 2021, Zelensky took the bull by the horns. On 2nd June, the President submitted a new bill to the Verkhovna Rada, under which the National Security and Defence Council would establish an 'oligarchs register.' The criteria for inclusion on the register were having a monopoly in a particular market, an income of at least one million times the Ukrainian poverty line of US$83 per month, influence on the Ukrainian media, and involvement in politics. Like public servants, oligarchs on the register would be required to declare their income. Registered oligarchs would also be prohibited from financing political parties or participating in the privatisation of Government property. In order to limit undesired influence, judges and ministers were also required to register their contact with oligarchs. Zelensky tweeted on 2nd July: 'The oligarchs are a thing of the past.'

Ihor Kolomoyskyi said he was prepared to be included on the register. Rinat Akhmetov's corporation, on the other hand, insisted that he was not an oligarch but an 'investor.' When the bill passed, Petro Poroshenko announced the sale of his three television channels 5 Kanal, Pryamiy and Espresso. 'The main reason they cooked up this "oligarchy bill" is to gain control of the media,' said a livid Poroshenko.

Anka Feldhusen, the German ambassador in Kyiv, called the bill a 'bold first step,' but added that it was 'mostly symbolic.' Feldhusen believed it was more important to finalise the judiciary reforms and to strengthen anti-corruption institutions. 'In the long term, the existing bodies simply need more powers, and greater support in the fight against the oligarchs.'

Ruslan Riaboshapka, the Prosecutor General who had been dismissed by Zelensky, analysed the oligarchy bill more cynically. He dug up the bill's explanatory memorandum, and posed the question of whether it provided any real benefit to ordinary citizens. Did it oblige the oligarchs to surrender even a part of their ill-gotten gains to the state? Riaboshapka could not find anything about that in the memorandum: 'What it mainly talks about is the President, the administrative body he has in his pocket [the Security Council] and the expansion of his own powers.'

On 22nd September, Zelensky was in New York for the Annual General Meeting of the United Nations. His telephone went off at 3am. In Kyiv, unknown assailants had opened fire on the car of his friend, advisor and business associate Serhiy Shefir. Shefir was unharmed, but his driver was wounded and taken to hospital. It was a deliberate attack, Zelensky was informed. From his hotel room, Zelensky recorded a short video. 'I don't know who's behind this,' he said, 'but getting my attention by shooting at my friend's car from the edge of the forest is pretty low. My response will be resolute.'

Zelensky's team speculated about who ordered the attack. The mild-mannered Shefir was not known to have any enemies – the conclusion was that it must have been a warning to Zelensky's own address. Perhaps the order had come from one of the mafia or smuggling bosses on the sanction list, or it could have been in response to the oligarchy bill.

The perpetrators were never identified. Within two weeks, however, the attack was forgotten and Ukraine had moved on to a different topic – President Zelensky's own integrity. On 3rd October, Kyiv theatre The Little Opera had planned to premiere the film *Offshore 95*. It was a documentary based on the Pandora Papers – a collection of over 11 million leaked documents from financial service providers. On 3rd October, in numerous countries, the International Consortium of Investigative Journalists began publishing exposés on the offshore accounts of hundreds of government employees across the world, including 35 national leaders. In their 2.9

terabytes of confidential data, Volodymyr Zelensky featured prominently. In *Offshore 95 – Secrets of Zelensky's Business*, Ukrainian journalists presented their findings.

But the premiere was called off at the last minute. Several hours before the scheduled screening, the cinema manager called journalists personally to tell them: 'We will not be showing the film on the President.' The manager then sent out a What'sApp message saying that the premiere could not go ahead due to renovations and faulty lights. The quality newspaper *Ukrainska Pravda* would later report that the manager had been contacted by a member of the SBU.

Within hours, the cancellation had snowballed into a huge scandal. The outrage was so great, in fact, that the film was screened that day after all.

Zelensky's offshore companies in Cyprus had already become public knowledge in 2019. New research by *Slidstvo.info* showed that the comedian, the Shefir brothers and another member of Kvartal 95 also had businesses on the British Virgin Islands and in Belize. At the heart of this complex corporate structure was the hitherto unknown Maltex Multicapital Corp, registered in the Virgin Islands.

The amount of money that was funnelled through it was considerable. It turned out that since 2012, Maltex Multicapital Corp had received $US40 million from businesses belonging to the powerful oligarch Ihor Kolomoyskyi.

The offshore network of Zelensky and his business partners owned three apartments in central London. One was located in Chalfont Court, a mansion block opposite 221B Baker Street, home of the fictional detective Sherlock Holmes. The second was yards away in Clarence Gate Gardens, an Art Nouveau-style block once home to poets, actors and composers and the third apartment in Westminster Palace Garden, five minutes' walk from the Houses of Parliament. It is real estate worthy of princes, with a total worth that amounted to US$7.5 million.

Shortly before the presidential elections, Zelensky had transferred his shares in Maltex Multicapital Corp to Serhiy Shefir. The purpose of the offshoring was unclear. Kolomoyskyi owned 1+1, the channel where Studio Kvartal 95 was under contract. But why had payments been made offshore? Was Zelensky guilty of tax evasion? Or had Studio Kvartal 95 helped to whitewash illicit takings for Kolomoyskyi's PrivatBank?

To allow Zelensky to present his side of the story, *Slidstvo. info* sent a list of detailed questions to the presidential office, but received no reply. Zelensky took until 17th October to address the matter during an interview. 'During Yanukovych's presidency, everybody moved their businesses across the border, especially in the TV world,' was his explanation. According to Zelensky, officials from the tax administration had visited him 'almost daily' during that time – a sign that the Government was looking for violations. Zelensky vehemently denied any whitewashing, but dodged the question of whether he had paid any tax.

Olena Loginova from *Slidstvo.info* was willing to give Zelensky the benefit of the doubt. But why did the offshore companies still exist? 'It implies that you have no confidence in the country where you originally built up your business, and the country that you now run,' said the journalist the following day. 'You are trying to hide something, and you must have a reason.'

On 27th October, the corruption watchdog NACP announced that it had investigated Zelensky's businesses and found nothing untoward. Less than two months later, however, a second scandal broke out, one that had lain dormant for far longer.

In July 2020, in a holiday resort close to the Belarusian capital of Minsk, 33 mercenaries were arrested. There were 32 Russians and one Belarusian. According to Belarusian President Lukashenko, Moscow had hired the men to destabilise the country in the lead-up to the presidential elections in August. However, Russian and Ukrainian media quickly reported the potential involvement of the Ukrainian secret services, and that Lukashenko may not have been the intended target. According to a Ukrainian journalist, Yuriy Butusov, the operation failed because Zelensky's staff had leaked information to Moscow. Vasyl Burba, head of the Ukrainian military security service (GUR), was supposedly fired by Zelensky because he wanted to interrogate the staff using a lie detector. The Ukrainian Government denied any involvement in the operation.

The issue was hotly discussed in the Ukrainian media and in broader society, especially when Christo Grozev, from the Bellingcat research collective, announced in 2020 that he would be producing a documentary about the scandal. Would there be any more surprises? Were there traitors in Zelensky's inner circle?

Although Grozev's documentary never came about, on 17th November 2021 Bellingcat released its inquiry into the Belarusian affair, and the report made shockwaves. It turned out that the Ukrainian secret services, the SBU and GUR, had set up a large-scale operation whose aim was to lure dozens of agents from the Russian mercenary company Wagner into a trap. The mercenaries had fought in the Donbas, and were thought to have much to say about Russia's role in the conflict. They might even have had more information on the downing of Malaysian Airlines flight MH17.

The Ukrainian secret services set up fake companies to hire Wagner's people as 'guards' for a job in Venezuela. The plan was to have the men travel to Minsk, where they would board a plane to Istanbul. While in Ukrainian airspace, however, the Turkish Airlines aircraft would be forced to land in Kyiv, where the mercenaries would be apprehended.

The plan was so brazen, it was almost destined to fail. But the person immediately responsible for the plan's failure was Zelensky himself. One day before the mercenaries' scheduled departure from Minsk, the Ukrainian President decided to postpone the operation. Thirty-two Wagner mercenaries were therefore taken to a holiday park to wait for the next flight, where their 'odd behaviour for Russian tourists' made them stick out like a sore thumb. Witnesses told the Belarusian police of athletic-looking men wearing military-style clothing who refused alcohol and stayed in their rooms on disco night.

'Wagnergate' came at a particularly inconvenient time. Over the course of 2021, Russia had started amassing enormous forces at the Ukrainian border. Both in Kyiv and in Western capitals, there was talk of imminent war. Some Ukrainians wondered out loud whether the Zelensky Government would be able to offer any resistance at all to the growing Russian threat.

To calm things down, Zelensky held a press conference on 26th November. The president explained that he ultimately decided against 'Operation Wagner' due to the enormous risks and many uncontrollable elements – such as the possibility that other passengers on board the aeroplane might sustain injuries, or the potential international scandal if a Turkish aircraft were to be hijacked in Ukrainian airspace.

The journalists were not immediately satisfied and asked a barrage of questions. The press conference lasted hours. The President looked exhausted.

'What is the likelihood of a war with Russia?' one reporter asked. 'As far as I know, we have already been at war for eight years,' said a moody Zelensky. 'We receive intelligence from various services daily, including those from partner countries who are supporting us.' He went on: 'We even have an audio recording of Ukrainians and Russians discussing Rinat Akhmetov's involvement in staging a Ukrainian coup.'

The journalists frantically started messaging and tweeting.

'I cannot tell you any more right now,' said Zelensky. 'But what I can tell you is that I am no Yanukovych. I'm not going to do a runner.'

8. The Wartime President

There is an unwritten law in Russian politics: whenever a Government department coordinates a complex operation, something is bound to go wrong. In Russian slang, such blunders are not uncommonly referred to using an English loan word: fakap.

On 18th February 2022, the Russian-appointed separatist leaders of Donetsk and Luhansk, Denis Pushilin and Leonid Pasechnik, published a video speech online. With grave expressions, the two men announced the evacuation of the citizenry. 'According to our information, the Ukrainian aggressor intends to march on the heart of our Republic,' said Pasechnik. 'To avoid civilian casualties, I urge all citizens to make for Russian territory as soon as possible.'

It was arrant disinformation: Ukraine had no intention of invading either Donetsk or Luhansk. When citizen investigators analysed the metadata attached to the video files, they saw straight away that they had been recorded two days earlier. The threat of the Ukrainian 'invasion' was clearly less acute than the leaders would have people believe.

This was not the only fakap. A Ukrainian activist, Serhiy Sternenko, ascertained that Pasechnik's video had been uploaded from a folder bearing the intriguing name: 'Attack of the Mongoose.'

The folder's title sounded suspiciously like a code name for a military operation. Ukrainian journalists recalled Operation Mongoose, a secret CIA programme from the 1960s aimed at unseating Cuban leader Fidel Castro. Others were reminded of Rikki-Tikki-Tavi, the grey mongoose from Rudyard Kipling's *The Jungle Book*. President Putin had expressed great admiration for the British author's work on several occasions, and cited from it during multiple public appearances.

Mongooses are so quick and agile, they can even do battle with the dreaded cobra. Their strategy is to disorient and exhaust their foe using feigned attacks and evasive manoeuvres, before striking out with lightning speed.

So what was Vladimir Putin's strategy? In the spring of 2021, Russia had begun to amass swarms of troops and artillery on the Ukrainian border. The West was concerned, and the Secretary General of NATO, Jens Stoltenberg, called Zelensky. On 22nd April, Russian defence minister Sergey Shoigu announced that the military 'exercises' were complete. Only a small portion of the troops had been recalled, however.

In September, tens of thousands of Russian soldiers trained in Belarus as part of a four-yearly military exercise, *Zapad* ('West'). Once complete, the number of troops on the border started growing again. In late January 2022, new 'exercises' in Belarus were announced, and Russian units began operating within 100km of Kyiv. One month later, the United States estimated that Russia had stationed 190,000 soldiers on the Ukrainian border. Washington, London and NATO in Brussels started speaking openly of a potential invasion.

Vladimir Putin's hands were free for a new military adventure. In mid-2020, via a heavily manipulated referendum, the Russian population had voted in favour of amending the constitution to grant Putin another potential two terms as President, until 2036. In August 2020, FSB agents made an attempt on opposition leader Alexey Navalny's life with a nerve agent, novichok. Navalny fell into a coma, but miraculously recovered after being airlifted to a hospital in Berlin. Upon returning to Moscow in 2021, he was arrested and imprisoned, much to the horror of the world at large. After that, both the movement he had founded and all remaining vestiges of opposition and independent media in Russia were systematically eradicated. By the end of the year, even the world-famous Russian human rights organisation Memorial was shut down.

Nearing 70, Vladimir Putin had become less and less interested in domestic politics. The former KGB agent from St. Petersburg now spoke mostly about other countries, geopolitics, and Russian history (rather, his revisionist version of it). The Russian president once described the dissolution of the Soviet Union as 'the greatest geopolitical catastrophe of the 20th Century.' In late 2021, he described the end of the Soviet empire as 'the disintegration of historic Russia.'

Was Putin planning to restore what he considered to be 'historic Russia'?

Over the preceding years, the Russian president had become increasingly interested in Belarus. In the late 1990s, Minsk and Moscow signed a framework agreement facilitating far-reaching reintegration of the two countries. With an ailing President Yeltsin at the helm in Moscow, the Belarusian President Alexander Lukashenko saw himself as the head of the new Bela-Russian union state. Ever since Putin's unexpected accession in 2000, Lukashenko had shown conspicuously little enthusiasm for the project. For the first two decades of his presidency, Putin left things as they were. Now, he was starting to put pressure on Belarus to finally take steps toward merging the two countries. Lukashenko had always delayed the process as much as possible, but massive protests in 2020 ultimately drove the dictator into Moscow's arms.

Putin's thoughts had also drifted toward Ukraine. In 2021, the Kremlin website published a long essay by Putin titled *On the Historic Unity of Russians and Ukrainians*. It was a pseudo-historical treatise with an imperialist message. In Putin's version of history, Russia was the only lawful heir of the Kyivan Empire, and all expressions of the Ukrainian language or culture were the wrongful consequence of foreign conquests by Poland, Lithuania or the Austro-Hungarian empire. Putin claimed that the unity of the 'great Russian nation' had been lost over the course of the centuries, and that from 1917 onwards, the Soviet authorities had further entrenched the division through the establishment of three separate republics for Russians, Belarusians, and Ukrainians.

In Putin's eyes, therefore, modern-day Ukraine was an anomaly. In his essay, he referred to the country derogatively as an 'anti-Russia project,' spurred on by the West. 'I am convinced that the true sovereignty of Ukraine can best be achieved through collaboration with Russia,' wrote the man who for seven straight years had been waging a clandestine war in the Donbas. 'We are one people, after all.'

While Russia's military movements were putting the world on edge, Putin suddenly seemed amenable to negotiation. In December 2021, Moscow proposed a new European security agreement to NATO, the details of which were immediately published on the website of the Russian ministry for Foreign Affairs – hardly a conventional channel for diplomatic communication. Russia demanded guarantees that Ukraine would never become a member of the North Atlantic Treaty Organisation (NATO), that its future expansion would be curtailed, and that all foreign NATO units in the 'new' eastern-European member states would be withdrawn.

The latter stipulation was particularly unacceptable to NATO, and so serious negotiations between the parties never got off the ground. However, NATO's rejection of Russia's proposals did give good cause for the Russian state media to report on the so-called 'NATO threat' in Ukraine. The implication was that Russia had to defend itself.

Plans for the Russian invasion had been in readiness for some time. They were not in the hands of the Russian armed forces, but the FSB. Over the previous years, the Fifth Service, run by General Sergey Beseda, had issued Putin with detailed reports of Ukraine's political and social development. The Bellingcat investigator Christo Grozev acquired unverified documents suggesting that Russia had spent billions on the formation of an underground network of informants and collaborators. In December 2021, according to the British security and defence think tank RUSI, the FSB had organised a programme of wargames directed by the Russian airborne units. The games simulated scenarios in which the vanguard of the imminent invasion – Russian *spetsnaz* (special units, or commandos) and airborne troops – could gain access to Ukrainian assets. The collaborators in the network would help them quickly grab crucial infrastructure and eliminate any Ukrainian administrators expected to offer resistance.

The Russian war plan strongly resembled the mongoose's tactics against the cobra. To create confusion, Russian troops would also enter Ukraine from multiple fronts, while elite troops struck in the heart of Kyiv. But Russia's plans were built on shaky ground. Christo Grozev Grozev stated that he had seen several reports by the FSB's Fifth Service with his own eyes. 'They're completely worthless,' he said. 'They told Putin that this was the right time to carry out such an operation, that Ukraine was politically unstable and that nobody would support the President.' Andrei Soldatov, an expert on the Russian intelligence services, confirmed that the FSB had painted far too rosy a picture for the Russian President: 'They merely wrote down what Putin wanted to read.'

On 29th January 2022, the *Washington Post* reported that American intelligence services held long-term suspicions that Putin was not being adequately apprised of the risks of an invasion. In an interview with the newspaper, an anonymous government officer described his astonishment at the Russian war preparations: 'To me, the idea of invading Ukraine and occupying it in any way, even temporarily, is extraordinarily ambitious and somewhat insane.'

In the New Year, the White House sounded the alarm bells with increasing urgency. Putin had already surprised the West once during the crisis of 2014, and the Biden administration now wished to mobilise public opinion against a potential Russian invasion. The American President clearly stated that although the United States would not intervene militarily, if Putin did invade Ukraine, Russia could certainly count on sanctions of unprecedented magnitude. To convince sceptical NATO partners, Biden gave the order to share unheard-of quantities of intelligence with other countries. At the same time, information was leaked to the press: American media channels reported almost daily on the signs of a Russian attack. On 26th January, Deputy Secretary of State Wendy Sherman even predicted an attack 'in mid-February.'

On 27th January, Joe Biden called Zelensky. That same day, a US news channel reported that the phone call 'did not go well.'

Zelensky had grave concerns too, but unlike Biden, he believed it was prudent to keep them to himself. The day after the phone call with the American President, he took some Western leaders to task regarding their 'undiplomatic' language: 'They just blurt out "Tomorrow will be war," without any regard for the potential panic it could cause in the markets or the financial sector.' Economic chaos would provide the perfect conditions for Moscow to orchestrate a violent upheaval, Ukrainian Government services warned. The mobilisation of armed forces would also be an ideal provocation for Putin to launch his invasion. Zelensky did not wish to goad Putin in any way. The President said to the media: 'I do not run my country the way yours is in the movie *Don't Look Up* [where an approaching meteor is ignored by the world]. We do look up. We know what's happening, we've been in this situation for eight years now.'

Meanwhile, behind the scenes, Zelensky was busy making war preparations. A team of American experts had advised Ukrainian forces to relocate their air defence systems, to prevent their immediate destruction by Russia's first attacks. Kyiv begged

Video appeal: *The Ukrainian President makes a direct appeal to Russian citizens for peace, 2022.*
IMAGO/ZUMA Wire

the West for more weapons, and received them. At Boryspil airport, pallet after pallet of British and American anti-tank missiles were unloaded daily from military transport planes.

The general belief within the Zelensky administration was that the Russian invasion would concentrate on the country's Russian-speaking regions: Kharkiv and the Donbas in the east, and Kherson in the south. 'The one thing we didn't anticipate were attacks from Belarus,' the National Security and Defence Council secretary Oleksiy Danilov later recalled. 'We did talk about it, but ultimately we reached a different conclusion.'

In late February, tensions rose even further.

On 21 February, Putin announced that the Russian Federation officially acknowledged the Donetsk and Luhansk People's Republics as 'independent states,' followed immediately by a statement that the Russian president would be sending 'peacekeeping troops' to the two regions.

That same day, according to Britain's RUSI, the commanders of the Russian airborne brigades were ordered to carry out a spectacular operation at the airport in Hostomel, a suburb of Kyiv 30km from Zelensky's presidential palace. Russian officers were frantically calling one another, and the flurry of activity had not gone unnoticed among Western espionage services. On 23rd February, *Newsweek* wrote that Washington had warned Zelensky once again, saying that the invasion could begin within 48 hours.

That same day, the Polish President, Andrzej Duda, was in Kyiv for a meeting with Zelensky. The Ukrainian President said he was certain his country would be invaded within a matter of hours, Duda recalled. 'The Russians think we won't fight back,' said Zelensky, 'but they are gravely mistaken.' At the end of their meeting, he said: 'Andrzej, this might be the last time we see one another.'

After seeing Duda, Zelensky consulted with all the party leaders in the Verkhovna Rada. The Ukrainian Parliament then voted to declare a state of emergency, thus granting the Government extraordinary powers. Shortly before midnight, a visibly fatigued Zelensky explained the decision, switching suddenly to Russian: 'Today I tried to call the President of the Russian Federation. I was met with total silence.' Then he addressed the citizens of Russia: 'We may have our differences, but that is no reason for us to be enemies. Listen to us, the Ukrainian people want peace.'

That night, at just after 4.30am, Olena Zelenska awoke to the sound of distant explosions. The bed beside her was empty. When she got up, she saw that her husband was already up and dressed. It was the last time he would be seen in a suit and tie. 'It has begun,' Zelensky said to his wife. He added that she needed to pack some things – clothes and passports – and that she should explain to Sasha and Kyrylo (aged 17 and 9) that war had broken out. Then he got into his car.

Zelensky was already at the presidential palace on Bankova Street in the centre of Kyiv when the head of the presidential staff, Andriy Yermak, arrived shortly before six. For months, Yermak and Zelensky had been preparing for a potential war, but right up until that moment, neither of them truly believed it would happen. Now the invasion was a reality.

After an initial barrage of cruise missiles, Russian troops flooded across the Ukrainian border on all sides: from the south, the north-east, and from Belarus towards the decommissioned Chernobyl nuclear power plant, en route to Kyiv.

One hour later, Russian President addressed the nation. Escalating violence in the Donbas had made intervention inevitable, Putin said. 'I have decided to execute a special military operation.' The aim, Putin claimed, was to 'demilitarise' and 'denazify' Ukraine, and to 'bring to justice' those Ukrainians who had committed war crimes against the populations of Donetsk and Luhansk. Putin thus revealed his endgame: a forced regime change in Kyiv.

As soon as it was light, 34 Russian helicopters flew hundreds of elite soldiers to Hostomel airport on the capital's north-eastern edge. Their task was to take over the airport, so that reinforcements could be flown in for a surprise attack on Kyiv. The Ukrainians had been forewarned, however, and heavy fighting broke out. Despite the resistance, the next day Russian soldiers headed for the city centre in small groups, looking for Zelensky.

The parliamentary chair, Ruslan Stefanchuk, who had succeeded Razumkov in October 2021, arrived at Bankova Street early in the morning to talk to Zelensky. 'He showed no fear,' he told *Time Magazine*. 'He was only surprised: How could this have happened?' Zelensky's staff were less collected, said Stefanchuk. 'We felt like the world was caving in around us.'

Stefanchuk hurried to the Rada to have the Parliament declare martial law. Later that day, Olena and the children joined Zelensky. But the presidential palace was not safe – Russian assassins were roaming the streets of Kyiv, bent on taking out the President. When darkness fell, armed skirmishes broke out around the palace. Zelensky's bodyguards turned off all the lights, and handed out bullet-proof vests and weapons to all staff. Most employees had never even seen an AK-47 close-up before, a presidential adviser, Oleksiy Arestovych, told *Time*. 'It was a madhouse.' Arestovych went on to say that the Russians attempted to storm the presidential palace twice that night.

While soldiers were barricading windows and doors with anything they could find, Zelensky was on the telephone receiving the latest intelligence from Washington and London. Kyiv was not safe, the British and Americans said, offering to evacuate Zelensky if he wished. Zelensky turned down the proposal, reportedly saying: 'The fight is here. I need ammunition, not a ride.' Zelensky also refused to be transported to a special security bunker close to Kyiv. Meanwhile, just outside the city, hundreds of Chechen fighters stood ready for a direct attack on the presidential palace. Gunfire broke out in the city centre as Ukrainian security agents sought out saboteurs and mercenaries.

Zelensky realised that he had to stay put. Prior to the outbreak of war, he had made the conscious decision to play down the threat to the Ukrainian people. Now that the Russians were on his doorstep, panic was a real possibility. In Kyiv there were long queues at the ATMs, and traffic on the exit roads had come to a standstill. In an attempt to further destabilise the situation, the next day Putin addressed the Ukrainian armed forces directly, claiming that the Zelensky administration was nothing more than a 'pack of junkies and neo-Nazis' and encouraging them to 'take power into their own hands.' The

Russian media spread the rumour that President Zelensky had disappeared, and was nowhere to be found.

Zelensky realised that he had to show himself to the nation. On the evening of 25th February, he slipped out with his closest members of staff – Prime Minister Denys Shmyhal, adviser Mykhailo Podolyak, chief of staff Andriy Yermak, and party leader Davyd Arakhamia. Clad in military green, the men stood before the presidential palace while Zelensky took a video with his phone, lit only by the street lights. 'The President is here,' said Zelensky: 'Our armed forces are here, our people are here. We will defend our independence, our country. Long live Ukraine!'

Volodymyr Zelensky was now 44 years old. When announcing his candidacy three years prior, he had promised to unseat the political elite, to root out corruption and to transform Ukraine into a modern and prosperous country – the Ukraine he had always dreamed of. Now the question was whether Ukraine could even continue to exist as an independent country.

Western military experts said that Ukraine could only defend itself against the Russian army – the second-strongest in the world – for a few days at most. But the Ukrainians stuck to their guns, and the Chechen fighters were obliterated before they even reached the capital.

Even during the first days of the war, Russia's advance on Kyiv suffered setbacks. Russian tanks found it difficult to manoeuvre in the wooded marshlands to the city's north, so the T-72s formed long convoys along the narrow asphalt roads, turning them into sitting ducks for small groups of Ukrainian soldiers armed with anti-tank missiles. Within two days, Kyiv's exit roads were blocked by blazing Russian armour, hampering the progress of other vehicles which then became easy pickings for the Ukrainian artillery. The Russians had no clear idea of where the Ukrainian defensive lines were, but thanks to a constant stream of US intelligence, Kyiv knew everything about the Russians.

The FSB believed that Ukraine's political elite was divided, and that one mighty blow would be enough to scatter the Government and force the army to surrender. But the opposite occurred. On the first day of the war, the former president Petro Poroshenko paid a visit to Zelensky. It was a meeting between nemeses. Ever since Zelensky's election, Poroshenko had been inundated with lawsuits. In January the Public Prosecutor demanded that the former president be taken into custody for 'high treason.' Now, however, the country's fate took precedence. 'I said: we have a common enemy, we need to work together,' said Poroshenko. 'Then we shook hands.'

Zelensky authorised the party leaders in the Rada to mobilise their support bases to offer resistance to the Russians. Within a few days, tens of thousands of AK-47s had been handed out in Kyiv alone. Ordinary Ukrainians, with no military training whatsoever, stood in line for hours to obtain a firearm.

The West, too, presented a united front. Both the United States and the European Union announced sanctions against Russia that few had considered possible. On 26th February, the West ejected Russian banks from the SWIFT global payment system. Beforehand, analysts had nicknamed this drastic measure the 'nuclear option,' however Western countries seemed prepared to go even further, freezing hundreds of billions in currency reserves that the Russian Central Bank had stored in international accounts. But the Russian economy was hit even harder when many Western companies, from French carmaker Renault to American pharmaceutical giant Johnson & Johnson, announced they were leaving Russia. The world-famous Moscow branch of McDonald's, which opened its doors on Pushkin Square in 1990, closed them.

Zelensky played a pivotal role in mobilising the international community. The Ukrainian President telephoned with the world, addressing national parliaments through an online video connection. He always did so clothed in an army-green T-shirt (showing off his now impressive biceps), and wrote all his speeches himself: no better author was to be found anywhere in Ukraine.

Zelensky addressed the European Parliament and the US Congress. He was the first foreign head of Government to address the Lower House of the Dutch Parliament. In Norway, he was the second – after Winston Churchill.

Knowing his audience: *Zelensky struck the right tone when speaking to assemblies around the world. In this picture, he addresses the UN Security Council on 24th April 2022*
IMAGO/ZUMA Press

Ukraine's President knew just how to strike the right tone. He echoed Churchill's World War II speeches when he told the UK Parliament: 'We will fight in the forests, in the fields, on the shores, in the streets.' To the Italian Parliament, he spoke of how the violence of war prevented Ukrainians from taking photographs of their laughing, happy children. When speaking to Indonesian diplomats, he reminded them of colonialism. To the Spanish Parliament, he brought up Guernica, and to Congress, he drew a comparison between the Russian invasion and the Japanese attack on Pearl Harbour in 1941. 'We have proven our strength,' Zelensky told the European Parliament on 1st March. 'So prove that you are with us. Prove that you will not abandon us. Prove that you indeed are Europeans. And then life will win over death, and light will win over darkness.' The world was impressed by the slight, charismatic President, who refused to be intimidated by the monstrous Russian war machine.

But Zelensky could also be hectoring – he was never satisfied, and continually raved that the West should supply even more weapons, impose even tougher sanctions. When NATO refused to institute a no-fly zone above Ukraine – which might have led to a direct military conflict with Russia – Zelensky responded emotionally. The President said in his daily video address: 'All the people who die from this day forward will also die because of you, because of your weakness.' To *CBS News*, he said: 'I am no longer interested in their diplomacy, that leads only to the destruction of my country.'

On 11 March 2022, when the war had already been underway for a little over two weeks, the intelligence expert, Andrei Soldatov, wrote that the FSB General Sergey Beseda and his deputy had been placed under house arrest due to poor management and the provision of bad intel. 'It finally seems to be dawning on Putin that his confidantes have led him into the abyss,' Soldatov wrote. Bellingcat's investigator Christo Grozev reported that at least 150 FSB officers had been relieved of their posts. Despite the fact that Russian tanks had reached Irpin, just north-west of Kyiv, and Brovary, a suburb on the Dnipro's eastern bank, surrounding the capital no longer seemed viable.

War crimes: *Visiting Bucha, the scene of alleged murder and torture of Ukrainian civilians, on 4th April 2022*
IMAGO/ZUMA *Wire*

Putin's Blitzkrieg had failed, and so the war became a longer, more drawn-out and grisly affair. Even from the very first day, Russia had drawn no distinction between military targets and the civilian population of Ukraine. Kharkiv, on the Russian border, was heavily bombarded. The industrial city of Mariupol on the Sea of Azov was systematically razed to the ground. Everywhere the Russian soldiers pillaged, raped and murdered. In Bucha, before the gates of Kyiv, hundreds of citizens were executed. In late March, the Prosecutor General, Iryna Venediktova, announced that her office had already registered 2,500 potential Russian war crimes. Zelensky could feel his people's suffering, and viewed all the gruesome footage himself. 'I see everything,' he said in an interview with the Australian current-affairs programme *60 Minutes*. 'Not only because I want to know what's going on, but because I want to share in the victims' lot.' Zelensky is not embarrassed to talk about his feelings when seeing the photographs of dead bodies. 'I feel hatred, I want vengeance,' he says. 'But once the initial flood of emotions has passed, hatred gives way to confusion. How can you treat people like this?'

Those in Zelensky's inner circle supported him all they could. Olena and the children were taken to safety, but the family still telephoned at dinner time via a special satellite connection. Everybody did their best to make jokes, Olena said.

Zelensky's colleagues from Kvartal 95 also tried to cheer him up. Olena Kravets sent a meme showing Chuck Norris, the unstoppable American martial-arts expert, on the phone with the Ukrainian president:

'Volodymyr? This is Chuck.'

Zelensky: 'How can I help you, Chuck?'

Zelensky recorded a video message nearly every day, to let the Ukrainians know he was still around. Very occasionally the country was treated to a glimpse of his comic talent, such as in the clip from 6th March, the day Russian state television aired an interview between Putin and an Aeroflot stewardesses. The editing shows that the meeting between the Russian President and the young women never took place (at one point Putin's hand passes right through the microphone on the table as though he were a ghost.) Zelensky mocked Putin at the end of a speech, proclaiming 'Long live Ukraine!' while deliberately moving the microphone past his face to the left.

After a month of fighting, Putin realised that the Ukrainian capital was out of his reach. On 29th March, Russia's deputy Defence minister, Alexander Fomin, announced Russia's decision to 'drastically reduce military activity directed at Kyiv and Chernihiv.' The next day, Moscow announced a new military objective: 'To complete the operation aimed at the total liberation of the Donbas.' The defeated Russian troops withdrew fully from Ukraine's north. Ukraine's general staff estimated Russian military casualties to be around 17,000. Washington put the number of Russian deaths at over 10,000. 'Unfortunately, the Russians have not yet fully understood just how robust the Ukrainian army is,' said Victoria Nuland, the US Under Secretary of State for Political Affairs.

The eastern relocation of the Russian operations ushered in a new stage of the conflict. The war in the Donbas became a war of attrition, with heavy losses on both sides. 'The situation is dire,' said Zelensky in late May. 'Every day, 60 to 100 soldiers perish in battle.' But Ukraine stood firm, and the nation's continued existence no longer seemed under threat.

Vladimir Putin had underestimated Zelensky, according to Oleksander Rodnyansky, founder of the Ukrainian television channel 1+1. In an interview with the BBC, the television magnate recalled his many years of collaboration with the former actor and comedian. 'I knew I was dealing with a very talented individual,' said Rodnyansky, 'but one who also had a strong personality. The Kremlin didn't do their homework: they failed to appreciate just how courageous he is.'

Rodnyansky went on to say that Ukrainians should consider themselves lucky to have someone like Zelensky to lead them through the war. 'This man is no coward, no thief, he has made no compromises, hasn't fled the country and has not surrendered. He's a fighter.'

'He has always stood for the truth, no matter what,' says Yevhen Koshovy, his former colleague and friend from Kvartal 95. 'We always believed in it. Now he is even more compelling, because he knows that all of Ukraine is standing behind him.'

On 3 June 2022, the 100th day of the war, Zelensky again stood before the presidential palace on Bankova Street to make a video – this time in broad daylight. Kyiv had become so safe that Western diplomats were returning to their embassies. It was a glorious morning, and the first lattes were being served at the city's cafés.

'The President is here,' said Zelensky. 'Our armed forces are here. And most importantly: our people are here. We have defended Ukraine for 100 days.'

A triumphant smile spread across his face. 'Victory is ours.'

A Note on Sources

This book draws from many hundreds of sources – books, newspaper articles, original press releases from media agencies, and interviews, in Ukrainian, Russian, and other languages. Before Zelensky became President, he was already a superstar; countless hours of online video footage are available on his life and work. The authors of this book invested a great deal of time in viewing this sometimes unedited source material.

In several instances, the authors have borrowed from Steven Derix's work as *NRC* media correspondent in Moscow and Ukraine. Many gems were unearthed by searching through archived webpages, such as the Kvartal 95 fan sites from the 1990s.

Volodymyr Zelensky and his colleagues from Kryvyi Rih are Russian-speaking; the President did not become fluent in Ukrainian until later in life. Nevertheless, this book uses Ukrainian forms of the names for Ukrainian places and people wherever possible. In doing so, the authors have gone a step further than the general practice of using Ukrainian except where a different (e.g. Russian) spelling has become standard, such as for 'Kiev' and 'Charkov.' In a time when Ukrainian independence is under constant threat of large-scale military violence, such alternative designations seemed inappropriate. For this reason, the authors decided on 'Kyiv' and 'Kharkiv,' as is becoming more customary throughout the English-speaking world.

The Ukrainian and Russian languages are written in the Cyrillic alphabet. While both a scientific and official transliteration exist, media in the English-speaking world use a plethora of different spellings. The authors of this book have tried to maintain a certain rigor in their spelling, but in some cases decided that common use is more important. Former heavy-weight Vitali Klitschko, who was based in Germany during his career, appears not as Klichko, but with his 'German' name. For the same reason, we spell the name of the incumbent president of Ukraine as 'Zelensky' and not 'Zelenskyi' or 'Zelenskyy'. The spelling 'Zelenskiy' reflects his name in Russian. Although Zelensky is Russian-speaking and learned Ukrainian only later in life, the authors felt it inappropriate to use this spelling.

When transliterating the Cyrillic script into legible English, the authors made grateful use of the excellent online engine transcriptor.nl, an initiative by Radboud University Nijmegen, the Dutch Language Union and the Institute for the Dutch Language.

This biography is not an academic publication, and therefore does not have footnotes or references. However, we have provided an extensive bibliography and list of sources.

Steven Derix and Marina Shelkunova

Bibliography

Sources in Dutch

Bezemer, J.W. & Jansen, Marc, *Een geschiedenis van Rusland* (Amsterdam 2015).

Derix, Steven, various articles, *NRC Handelsblad* (2014-2022).

Jansen, Marc, Grensland. *Een geschiedenis van Oekraïne*, (Amsterdam 2014).

Interview with president Zelensky, *Nieuwsuur* (27 May 2022).

Sources in English

Amanpour, Christiane & Lyons, Emmet, "'The number one target is all of us": First Lady Olena Zelenska warns no one in Ukraine is safe from Russian forces', *CNN* (13 April 2022).

Applebaum, Anne & Goldberg, Jeffrey, 'Liberation without victory. In a wide-ranging conversation at his compound in Kyiv, Ukrainian President Volodymyr Zelensky tells *The Atlantic* what Ukraine needs to survive – and describes the price it has paid', *The Atlantic* (15 April 2022).

Barnes, Julian E. & Cooper, Helene, 'U.S. Battles Putin by Disclosing His Next Possible Moves', *New York Times* (13 February 2022).

Barnes, Julian E. a.o., 'U.S. Intelligence Is Helping Ukraine Kill Russian Generals', *New York Times* (4 May 2022). 'Biden declassified Russia intel due to allied 'skepticism', U.S. spy chief says', *CNN* (6 June 2022).

Bo Lillis, Katie & Liptak, Kevin, 'U.S. officials say Russia has list of senior Ukrainian officials it would remove if it invades', *CNN* (18 February 2022).

Brennan, David a.o., 'Exclusive: U.S. Warns Ukraine of Full-Scale Russian Invasion Within 48 Hours', *Newsweek* (23 February 2022).

Chance, Matthew & Herb, Jeremy, 'Ukrainian official tells CNN Biden's call with Ukrainian President "did not go well" but White House disputes account', *CNN*, (28 January 2022).

Corruption Perceptions Index, *Transparency International* (2019)

Detsch, Jack a.o., 'Russia Planning Post-Invasion Arrest and Assassination Campaign in Ukraine, U.S. Officials Say', *Foreign Policy* (18 February 2022).

Devan, Cole, 'Zelensky: "I'm ready for negotiations" with Putin, but if they fail, it could mean "a third World War"', *CNN* (20 March 2022).

EU Anti-Corruption Initiative in Ukraine, 'Constitutional crisis: a year later' (27 October 2021).

'Exclusive interview with Ukraine President Volodymyr Zelensky', *60 Minutes Australia, Nine Network* (01 May 2022).

Gorchinskaya, Katya, 'A brief history of corruption in Ukraine: the Yanukovych era', *Eurasianet* (3 June 2020).

Halifax International Security Forum, 'Halifax Chat: President Petro Poroshenko' (2019).

Harris, Shane a.o., 'U.S. and allies debate the intelligence on how quickly Putin will order an invasion of Ukraine – or whether he will at all', *The Washington Post* (29 January 2022).

Horovitz, David, 'A serious man: Zelensky bids to address Ukraine's dark past, brighten its future', *The Times of Israel* (19 January 2020).

'How Russia's mistakes and Ukrainian resistance altered Putin's war', *Financial Times* (18 March 2022).

Lee Matthew & Merchant, Nomaan, 'American spy agencies review their misses on Ukraine, Russia', *Associated Press News* (4 June 2022).

Loginova, Elena, 'Pandora Papers Reveal Offshore Holdings of Ukrainian President and his Inner Circle', *Organized Crime and Corruption Reporting Project* (03 October 2021).

Osborn, Andrew & Ostroukh, Andrey, 'Putin rues Soviet collapse as demise of "historical Russia"', *Reuters* (12 December 2021).

Pelley, Scott, 'The wartime president: Ukrainian President Volodymyr Zelenskyy speaks with Scott Pelley in Kyiv', *60 Minutes, CBS News* (10 April 2022).

Reynolds, Nick & Watling, Jack, 'The Plot to Destroy Ukraine', *Royal United Services Institute* (5 February 2022).

Reynolds, Nick & Watling, Jack, 'Operation Z: The Death Throes of an Imperial Delusion', *Royal United Services Institute* (22 April 2022).

Roth Andrew & Walker Shaun , 'Volodymyr Zelenskiy: "My White House invitation? I was told it's being prepared"', *The Guardian* (7 March 2020).

Shuster, Simon, 'Inside Zelensky's World', *Time* (28 April 2022).

Shuster, Simon, '"I'm Not Afraid of the Impeachment Questions": How Ukrainian President Volodymyr Zelensky Is Navigating His Role in the World's Biggest Political Drama', *Time* (5 December 2019).

Singhvi, Anjali a.o., 'How Kyiv Has Withstood Russia's Attacks', *New York Times* (2 April 2022).

Sonne, Paul, 'Russian troop movements near Ukraine border prompt concern in U.S., Europe', *The Washington Post* (30 October 2021).

Tapper, Jack, 'Interview with President of Ukraine Volodymyr Zelensky', *CNN* (17 April 2022).

Terterov, Marat, *Doing Business with Ukraine* (third edition), *Global Market Briefings Series* (2004).

Trofimov, Yaroslav, 'Ukraine's Special Forces Hold Off Russian Offensive on Kyiv's Front Lines', *Wall Street Journal* (4 March 2022).

Waal, Thomas de, 'Fighting a Culture of Corruption in Ukraine', Carnegie Europe (18 December 2016).

'White House says Ukrainian President Zelensky is "downplaying the risk of invasion"', *Fox News* (29 January 2022).

'Why is reform hard in Ukraine?', Atlantic Council, online meeting, YouTube (5 November 2020).

World Economic Forum, *The Global Competitiveness Report* (2019).

Yekelchyk, Serhy, *Ukraine: Birth of a Modern Nation* (2007); second edition (2015-2020).

Zentrum Liberale Moderne, 'Sanctions against Viktor Medvedchuk and his allies' (2 March 2021).

Sources in Polish

Czupryn, Anita a.o., 'Andrzej Duda w wywiadzie dla "Polski Times": "Ważne byśmy się liczyli na arenie międzynarodowej"', *Polska Times* ['Andrzej Duda in an interview with *Polska Times*: "It is important that we can count on the international community"'] (19 May 2022).

Sources in Ukrainian

'100 найбагатших українців 2021', *Forbes* ['The hundred richest Ukrainians 2021'] (6 May 2021).

'100 днів президента Володимира Зеленського', *1+1* ['100 days of president Volodymyr Zelensky'] (31 August 2019).

Antrim, Taylor, 'Перша леді України – про війну, яка змінила світ, і світ, який може пришвидшити перемогу', *Vogue Ukraine* ['The First Lady of Ukraine on the war, how the world has changed, and how the world can bring itself closer to victory'] (8 April 2022).

Kundra, Ondřej & Brolík, Tomáš, 'Зло не абсолютне, добро переможе. Ексклюзивне інтерв'ю з першою леді України Оленою Зеленською',

Respekt ['Evil is not absolute, good will triumph. An exclusive interview with the First Lady of Ukraine, Olena Zelenska'] (19 April 2022).

'Акція протесту під стінами КСУ', *24 Канал* ['Act of protest below the walls of the Constitutional Court of Ukraine', *Kanal 24*] (30 October 2020).

'Арсен Аваков вперше і відверто після відставки', *Україна 24* ['Arsen Avakov speaks for the first time after his resignation', *Ukraina 24*] (4 November 2022).

Алеканкіна, Ксенія & Тищук, Тетяна, 'Промайнув як мить: що встиг уряд Гончарука за півроку?', *Вокс Україна* [Alekaninka, Ksenia & Tishchuk, Tetyana, 'Gone in a flash: what has the Honcharuk government achieved in six months?', *Vox Ukraina*] (5 March 2020).

Андрейковець, Костя, 'СБУ підтвердили, що встановили прослуховування біля офісу Зеленського. Вони заявляють, що за ним не стежать', *Бабель* [Andreykovets, Kostia, 'The SBU confirms it installed wiretaps near Zelensky's office, but claims not to be monitoring him', *Babel*] (4 March 2019).

Андрейковець, Костя, 'Ми не працюємо в Росії». Зеленський відповів «Схемам» та «про всяк випадок вибачився', *Бабель* [Andreykovets, Kostia, '"We do not work in Russia". Zelensky responds to programme "Schemes" and apologises "for any potential situations"', *Babel*] (8 January 2019).

Андрейковець, Костя & Жартовська, Марія, '"Це погано". Разумков прокоментував відмову підтримати санкції проти каналів Медведчука', *Бабель* [Andreykovets, Kostia & Zhartovska, Maria, '"It's just not right".

Razumkov comments on the sanctions announced against Medvedchuk's TV channels', *Babel*] (3 February 2021).

Андрейковець, Костя а.о., 'Саміт 'нормандської четвірки' в Парижі: Володимир Зеленський обговорив з Володимиром Путіним, Емманюелем Макроном і Ангелою Меркель конфлікт на Донбасі і обмін полоненими. Текстова онлайн-трансляція', *Бабель* [Andreykovets, Kostia, a.o., 'The Normandy Format summit in Paris: Volodymyr Zelensky speaks with Vladimir Putin, Emmanuel Macron and Angela Merkel about the conflict in the Donbas and the exchange of war prisoners', Liveblog, *Babel*] (09 December 2019).

Балачук, Ірина, 'Порошенко розповів, скільки є справ проти нього, і хто за цим стоїть', *Українська правда* [Balachuk, Iryna, 'Poroshenko reveals how many cases have been brought against him, and by whom', *Ukrainska Pravda*] (1 July 2020).

Безпалько, Уляна & Лєліч, Мілан, 'Трупові ігри. Що відбувається в "Слузі народу" і хто її контролює', *РБК-Україна* [Bezpalko, Yuliana & Lelich, Milan, 'Group games. What happens at "Servant of the People" and who controls the party', *RBK-Ukraina*] (1 February 2021).

Брифінг президента Зеленського за участю іноземних ЗМІ, *ТСН* [Briefing by president Zelensky with participation by the international media, *The TV-News*] (28 January 2022).

'"Будь сильним, тримайся": українські військові стали на захист Зеленського, *РБК-Україна* ['"Be strong, keep going": Ukrainian soldiers support Zelensky', *RBK-Ukraina*] (30 November 2017).

'Буковинські зіркові зустрічі', Володимир Зеленський ч.1, ч. 2, YouTube ['Encounters with stars in Bukovyna', Volodymyr Zelensky, parts 1 and 2] (2013).

Бутченко, Максим, 'Колишні Зеленського. П'ять звільнених топчиновників — про плюси і мінуси президента і перспективу реформ в Україні', *HB* [Buchenko, Maksym, 'Zelensky's exes. Five former top officials on the president's strengths and weaknesses, and the prospects for reform in Ukraine', *NV*] (8 November 2020).

Бюллетень Свобода слова. Спецвипуск 51, Харківська правозахисна група [Overview of freedom of speech. Special report 51, Kharkiv Human Rights Protection Group] (2000).

'В Україні щоденна кількість щеплень проти COVID-19 має зрости до 350 тисяч', Офіс Президента України ['In Ukraine, the daily COVID-19 vaccination rate needs to rise to 350,000', Office of the President of Ukraine] (2 November 2021).

'В.Зеленський - про концерт в зоні АТО', *Сніданок з 1+1* ['V. Zelensky on his concert in the ATO-zone', *Breakfast with 1+1*] (21 August 2014).

'Вбити Не Можна Лякати', *Свобода слова Савіка Шустера* ['You can't be afraid to kill', *Free Speech with Savik Shuster*] (24 September 2022).

'Вбити боротьбу з корупцією. Як Конституційний Суд повертає бандитські 90-ті', *Українська правда* ['Death to the fight against corruption. How the Constitutional Court is bringing back the mafia 90s', *Ukrainska Pravda*] (29 October 2020).

'Венеційська комісія радить Україні змінити закон про Конституційний суд', *Європейська Правда* ['The Venice Commission advises Ukraine to change the law for the Constitutional Court', *Evropeiska Pravda*] (10 December 2020).

'Вишинський та Цемах входять до складу осіб, яких відправили до РФ для обміну', *ТСН* ['Vyshynsky, and Tsemakh are part of the group sent to Russia for a prisoner exchange', *The TV-News*] (7 September 2019).

'Вибори президента України. Марафон ТСН', *ТСН* ['The Ukrainian presidential elections. The TSN marathon', *The TV-News*] (21 April 2019).

'Відсторонення Тупицького: КСУ проведе збори 5 січня', *Укрінформ* ['Tupytsky's dismissal, the Constitutional Court convenes on 5 January', *Ukrinform*] (30 December 2020).

'Володимир Зеленський закликав Януковича врозумітись', *ТСН* ['Volodymyr Zelensky urges Yanukovych to show understanding', *The TV-News*] (1 March 2014).

'Володимир Зеленський схуднув на 6 кг заради ролі, *1+1* ['Volodymyr Zelensky lost 6 kilos for his role'] (14 August 2017).

'Володимир Зеленський: За два роки в межах програми "Велике будівництво" оновлено й побудовано понад 40% основної мережі доріг України', Офіс Президента України ['Volodymyr Zelensky: as part of the "Great Building" programme, over 40 per cent of Ukraine›s main road network will be resurfaced.' Office of the President of Ukraine] (24 December 2021).

Воробйова, Анна, 'Акторка Олена Кравець: Зеленський досі читає та перевіряє жарти в чатах 'Кварталу 95', *Бабель* [Vorobyova, Anna, 'Actress Olena Kravets: Zelensky continues to read and monitor jokes in Kvartal 95 chats', *Babel*] (6 October 2019).

Войтенко, Костя & Колесниченко, Марина, 'Володимир Зеленський дав карантинну пресконференцію. Про що говорив президент понад три години – у текстовій трансляції 'Бабеля', *Бабель* [Voytenko, Kostia & Kolesnichenko, Maryna, 'Volodmyr Zelensky gives a quarantine press conference. What the president has been talking about for three years – in Babel's text broadcast', *Babel*] (20 May 2020).

Ворона, Валерій (ed.), Українське суспільство: моніторинг соціальних змін. 30 років незалежності. Випуск 8 [Vorona, Valeri (ed.), *Ukrainian society: monitoring of social change. Thirty years of independence*. Edition 8] (Kyiv, 2021).

'Головні дебати країни: Зеленський – Порошенко', *Zelenskyy President* (YouTube channel) ['The country's most important debate: Zelensky versus Poroshenko'] (19 April 2017).

'Держкіно чекає документи на заборону 'Сватів', *Укрінформ* ['The Ukrainian State Film Agency is waiting for documentation to axe *Svaty*', *Ukrinform*] (24 November 2017).

Добуш, Юстина, 'Всі у захваті від нього? Історія успіху Студії «Квартал-95», *Hromadske* [Dobush, Justyna, 'Is everybody happy with him? The success story of Studio Kvartal 95'] (8 April 2019).

Ексклюзив ЖВЛ: з якими труднощами зіткнулась Олена Зеленська у статусі першої леді, *Життя відомих людей* [ZhVL exclusive: The hardships experienced by Olena Zelenska as First Lady, *The Lives of Famous People*] (25 September 2019).

'Етапи дорослішання. Що змінилося в житті і в свідомості українців за 26 років незалежності', *НВ* ['Stages of maturity. What has changed in the life and consciousness of Ukrainians during 26 years of independence?', NV] (24 August 2017).

'Є ознаки узурпації влади: заява правозахисних організацій щодо санкцій проти громадян України', Харківська правозахисна група ['Signs of a takeover: statement by human rights organisations on the sanctions against Ukrainian citizens', Kharkiv Human Rights Protection Group] (6 April 2021).

'Євросоюз: Україна має право боротися з каналами Медведчука, але є межі', *Європейська Правда* ['EU: Ukraine has the right to take action against Medvedchuk's TV stations, but there are limits', *Evropeiska Pravda*] (3 February 2021).

Жартовська, Марія, '25 днів до виборів президента. Зеленський провів закриту зустріч з іноземними журналістами. Ми дізналися, про що вони розмовляли', *Бабель* [Zhartovska, Maria, '25 days before the presidential elections, Zelensky held a private meeting with international journalists. We find out what they talked about', *Babel*] (06 March 2019).

'За крок до миру', *Zelenskyy President* (YouTube channel) ['A step towards peace'] (27 October 2019).

Звернення Президента України Володимира Зеленського до італійців та усіх європейців, Офіс Президента України [Speech by the president of Ukraine for the Italians and all other Europeans, Office of the President of Ukraine] (12 March 2022).

Звернення Президента України щодо ситуації з протидією коронавірусу, Офіс Президента України [Speech by the president of Ukraine on combating COVID-19, Office of the President of Ukraine] (29 March 2020).

'Зеленський про конституційну кризу', *Свобода слова* ['Zelensky on the constitutional crisis', *Free Speech*] (2 November 2020).

'Зеленський прокоментував офшори 95 Кварталу: Чесно кажучи, сюжет не дуже', *Свобода слова* ['Zelensky comments on the offshore holdings of Kvartal 95: Honestly, that's all it is', *Free Speech*] (18 October 2021).

'Зеленський планує в Брюсселі вручити орден віцепрезиденту Єврокомісії', *Європейська Правда* ['Zelensky plans to issue an honour to the vice-president of the European Commission', *Evropeiska Pravda*] (5 October 2020).

'Зеленський має право розпустити Конституційний суд – представник президента в КСУ Веніславський', *Радіо Свобода* ['Zelensky has the right to disband the Constitutional Court, says the Court's presidential representative, Venislavsky', *Radio Svoboda*] (11 November 2020).

'Зелена родина ру'. Кінобізнес Зеленського у *Росії*' *Радіо Свобода* ['The green fatherland.ru, Zelensky's film business in Russia', *Radio Svoboda*] (17 January 2019).

'Зробили з РНБО якогось інквізитора': Данілов відповів на претензії

Кличка, *Unian* ['They are turning the NSDC into an inquisitor: Danilov responds to allegations by Klitschko'] (24 August 2021).

'Зустріч Зеленського з представниками іноземних ЗМІ', *ICTV* ['Zelensky's meeting with international media representatives'] (28 January 2022).

'Зустріч Президента України Володимира Зеленського з представниками іноземних ЗМІ', Офіс Президента України ['President of Ukraine Volodymyr Zelensky's meeting with international media representatives', Office of the President of Ukraine] (12 March 2022).

'Інтерв'ю з першою леді України Оленою Зеленською', *Vogue Ukraine* ['Interview with the First Lady of Ukraine, Olena Zelenska'] (18 November 2019).

Інтерв'ю Зеленського: Президент розповів про зустріч з Байденом і Путіним, ставлення до Порошенка і долю олігархів, *ТСН* [Interview with Zelensky: the president talks about his meetings with Biden and Putin, relations with Poroshenko and the fate of the oligarchs, *The TV-News*] (24 June 2021).

Інавгурація Володимира Зеленського, *ТСН* [Inauguration of Volodymyr Zelensky, *The TV-News*] (20 May 2019).

Інтерв'ю Володимира Зеленського проекту 60 Minutes австралійського телеканалу Nine Network, Офіс Президента України [Volodymyr Zelensky's interview with *60 Minutes Australia*, Office of the President of Ukraine] (2 May 2022).

Інтерв'ю Володимира Зеленського журналісту грецького суспільного мовника ERT, Офіс Президента України [Volodymyr Zelensky›s interview with a journalist from Greek public TV station ERT, Office of the President of Ukraine] (2 May 2022).

Калюжна, Анна & Юрченко, Аліса, 'Хто з депутатів в Раді найактивніше відстоює інтереси Ахметова і Коломойського', *Bihus.Info* [Kalyuzhna, Anna & Jurchenko, Alisa, 'Which Rada delegates have most actively represented the interests of Akhmetov and Kolomoyskyi'] (12 January 2021).

Карякина, Ангелина & Кутепов, Богдан, 'Теніс, бар і '95 квартал': день у штабі Зеленського, *Hromadske* [Karyakyna, Angelyna & Kutepov, Bohdan, 'Ping pong, drinks and Kvartal 95: a day in the life of Zelensky's election staff'] (21 April 2019).

'Керівник Венеційської комісії відреагував на законопроєкт Зеленського стосовно КС', *Українська правда* ['The President of the Venice Commission responds to Zelensky's proposed bill on the Constitutional Court', *Ukrainska Pravda*] (31 October 2021).

Климська, Вероніка, 'Як українці стали мільйонерами: сумний досвід 90-х – фото, *24 Канал* [Klymska, Veronika, 'How Ukrainians became billionaires: a sad tale from the nineties – with photos', *Kanal 24*] (2 July 2020).

'Кошовий про Зеленського: Він завжди був таким', *Телемарафон UAразом* ['Koshovy on Zelensky: he has always been like that', *TV-marathon UArazom*] (16 March 2022).

Кошкіна, Соня & Базар, Олег, 'Юрій Луценко: Перші гроші в донецьку олігархію завіз Кобзон – з рук кемеровської мафії', *LB.ua* [Koshkina, Sonia & Bazar, Oleh, 'Yuriy Lutsenko: Kobzon brought the first money to the Donetsk oligarchs – from the Kemerovo mafia'] (30 September 2021).

Красінський, Владислав, 'Пан Секретар. Яку роль Олексій Данілов грає у команді президента', *РБК- Україна* [Krasinsky, Vladyslav, 'Mister secretary. What is Oleksiy Danilov's role on the president's team?' *RBK-Ukraina*] (13 July 2021).

Кравець, Роман & Сарахман, Ельдар, 'Володимир Зеленський: 1 квітня – офігенний день для перемоги клоуна', *Українська правда* [Kravets, Roman & Sakharman, Eldar, 'Volodymyr Zelensky: 1 April is a tremendous day for the clown's victory', *Ukrainska Pravda*] (21 January 2019).

Кравець, Роман, 'Олександр Пікалов: Я не бачу для Зеленського шляху назад у 'Квартал', *Українська правда* [Kravets, Roman, 'I do not see any way back to Kvartal for Zelensky', *Ukrainska Pravda*] (25 October 2021).

Кравець, Роман а.о., 'Хотів заразитися коронавірусом. Два дні з президентом Зеленським', *Українська правда* [Kravets, Roman, a.o., 'I wanted to infect myself with coronavirus. Two days with president Zelensky', *Ukrainska Pravda*] (9 June 2020).

Кізілов, Євген 'Проти Порошенка вже відкрили 58 кримінальних справ – адвокати', *Українська правда* [Kizilov, Yevhen, 'Lawyers: 58 lawsuits already filed against Poroshenko', *Ukrainska Pravda*] (18 September 2020).

Кузьменко, Євген, 'Дмитро Разумков: "Більшу частину питань, що розглядаються, ми бачимо в останній момент перед нарадою РНБО.

По-іншому воно, на жаль, не працює'", *Цензор. нет* [Kuzmenko, Yevhen, 'Dmytro Razumkov: "We have noticed that we are not presented with the matters to be discussed in the NSDC until the last minute. Unfortunately, there is no other way"', Censor.net] (2 April 2021).

Кузьменко, Євген, 'Віцеспікерка ВР Олена Кондратюк: "Зараз, на жаль, відбувається імітація парламентаризму. Виглядає, що парламент втрачає велику суб'єктність, яку він мав усі роки"', *Цензор. нет* [Kuzmenko, Yevhen, 'Rada vice-chair Olena Kondratiuk: "Sadly, right now we are seeing an imitation of parliamentary democracy. The parliament seems to be losing the substance it had for all those years"', Censor.net] (1 June 2021).

Литвин, Володимир, 'Акт Проголошення Незалежності України', *Енциклопедія історії України* [Lytvyn, Volodymyr, 'Ukraine's declaration of independence', *Historical Encyclopedia of Ukraine*] (Kyiv 2003).

Мельник, Олена , 'У Раді розпалася коаліція. З неї вийшла фракція 'Народний фронт', Бабель [Melnik, Olena, 'The coalition in the Rada has fallen apart. The People's Front party has left', *Babel*] (17 May 2019).

Мельник, Олена, "'Буде ініціювати". Радник Зеленського назвав причини для розпуску Ради', *Бабель* [Melnik, Olena, "'I will get to work on it." Zelenksy's adviser lists the reasons behind the dissolution of the Rada', *Babel*] (17 May 2019).

Мельник, Олена, 'Фірми на Кіпрі, орендована квартира в Британії та Land Rover. Зеленський вперше показав свою декларацію', *Бабель* [Melnik, Olena, 'Companies in Cyprus, a rental apartment in Great Britain and a Land Rover. Zelensky declares his assets for the first time', *Babel*] (25 January 2019).

Мельник, Олена, 'Зеленський вийшов зі складу кіпрської компанії', *Бабель* [Melnik, Olena, 'Zelensky gives up his shares in Cypriot company', *Babel*] (24 January 2019).

'Моніторинг електоральних настроїв українців: січень 2019', Соціологічна група Рейтинг ['Monitoring the electoral preferences of Ukrainians, January 2019', Sociological Rating Group] (31 January 2019).

'НАБУ відкрило справу проти Нефьодова', *РБК- Україна* ['NABU opens case against Nefyodov', *RBK- Ukraina*] (4 March 2020).

'Наші вдома. Як українські полонені поверталися на Батьківщину', *Zelenskyy President* (YouTube channel) ['Our boys are coming home. How the Ukrainian prisoners of war returned to the fatherland'] (11 September 2019).

'"Навіть бабусі брали каміння". Евакуйована з Уханя українка заявила, що її шокували протести у Нових Санжарах', *НВ* ["Even grandmas threw stones". An evacuee from Wuhan tells of how shocked she was at the protests in Novi Sanzhary', *NV*] (21 February 2020).

'На засіданні РНБО Президент України дав доручення невідкладно зареєструвати у Верховній Раді законопроект, у якому передбачається відновлення доброчесності судочинства у Конституційному Суді', Офіс Президента України ['During a session of the National Security and Defence Council, the president of Ukraine ordered that a bill proposal be immediately submitted to the Verkhovna Rada to restore the integrity of proclamations by the Constitutional Court', Office of the President of Ukraine] (19 February 2022).

'О. Данілов: Указ Президента України, яким уведено в дію рішення РНБО на підтримку децентралізації, є фундаментальним у взаєминах центральної та місцевої влади, РНБОУ, rnbo.gov.ua ['O. Danilov: the decree by the President of Ukraine, which put into effect the decision of the NSDC to support decentralization, is of fundamental importance to the relations between the central and local authorities'] (13 August 2021).

'Олена Зеленська: інтерв'ю для VIP з Наталією Мосейчук', *TCH* [Olena Zelenska, interview for VIPs by Natalia Moseichuk, *The TV-News*] (13 May 2021).

'Олігархи в законі. Кого хоче 'розкуркулити' Зеленський', *Українська правда* ['Oligarchs of the underworld. Who does Zelensky want to "de-kulakise"?', *Ukrainska Pravda*] (3 June 2021).

Панфілович, Олег, 'Зеленський поскаржився поліції, що за ним стежать. Правоохоронці почали розслідування', *Бабель* [Panfilovych, Oleh, 'Zelensky reports being monitored to the police. The judiciary launches an investigation', *Babel*] (7 February 2019).

Петренко, Роман, '"Ми не вірили до останнього": Єрмак розповів про їхні з Зеленським перші години війни', *Українська правда* [Petrenko, Roman, '"We couldn't believe it until the last moment": Yermak tells of his first hours of the war with Zelensky', *Ukrainska Pravda*] (10 March 2020).

Перелік фізичних та юридичних осіб стосовно яких застосовані обмежувальні заходи (санкції), РНБОУ, rnbo.gov.ua [List of natural and legal persons subject to restrictive measures (sanctions), NSDC, rnbo.gov.ua] (2017-2021).

Підсумки-2018: громадська думка, Фонд 'Демократичні ініціативи' імені Ілька Кучеріва & Центр Разумкова [2018 Results: opinion polls, the Ilka Kucheriv 'Democratic Initiatives' Foundation & Razumkov Centrre] (28 December 2018).

'Пресмарафон Зеленського на Kyiv Food Market', *Hromadske* ['Zelensky's press marathon at the Food Market in Kyiv'] (10 October 2019).

Президент України – про посилення обороноздатності держави, Офіс Президента України [The president of Ukraine on strengthening national defence, Office of the President of Ukraine] (24 February 2022).

Президент України Володимир Зеленський поспілкувався з представниками західних ЗМІ, Офіс Президента України [President Zelensky spoke with representatives of the western media, Office of the President of Ukraine] (03 March 2022).

Президент України підписав указ про відсторонення Олександра Тупицького від посади судді Конституційного Суду строком на два місяці, Офіс Президента України [The president of Ukraine signs a decree to suspend Oleksander Tupytsky from the position of judge at the Constitutional Court for a period of two months. Office of the President of Ukraine] (29 December 2021).

Прес-конференція Володимира Зеленського для представників українських і міжнародних ЗМІ, Офіс Президента України [Press conference by Volodymyr Zelensky for representatives of the Ukrainian and international press, Office of the President of Ukraine] (23 April 2022).

'Прес-марафон за участю Володимира Зеленського "30 запитань Президенту України"', Офіс Президента України ['Press marathon with Volodymyr Zelensky "thirty questions for the president of Ukraine"', Office of the President of Ukraine] (26 November 2021).

Проект Закону про відновлення суспільної довіри до конституційного судочинства, Верховна Рада України, rada.gov.ua [Proposed bill for restoring public confidence in the Constitutional Court, Verkhovna Rada of Ukraine] (9 October 2020).

Проскуряков, Самуїл , 'Біжи, або помреш. В 90-х у Кривому Розі підлітки організовували банди та вбивали один одного – Заборона розповідає їхню історію', *Zaborona* [Proskuryakov, Samuil, 'Run or die. In the nineties, teenagers formed gangs and murdered each other – Zaborona tells their story'] (15 September 2020).

Промова Президента України Володимира Зеленського перед Конгресом США, Офіс Президента України [Speech by president Volodymyr Zelensky to the United States Congress, Office of the President of Ukraine] (16 March 2022).

Промова Президента України Володимира Зеленського перед Конгресом США, Офіс Президента України [Speech by president Volodymyr Zelensky to the Norwegian Parliament, Office of the President of Ukraine] (30 March 2022). (30 March 2022).

'Порошенко сам фінансував свою виборчу кампанію', *Українська правда* ['Poroshenko funded his own election campaign', *Ukrainska Pravda*] (01 May 2019).

'Роднянський: 'Росіянам потрібна національна катастрофа', *BBC News Україна* ['Rodnyansky: the Russians need a national catastrophe', *BBC News Ukraine*] (May 2022).

'Розв'язана Росією війна проти України впливає на глобальну ситуацію – звернення Президента України до співтовариства Foreign Policy Community of Indonesia (FPC)', Офіс Президента України ['Russia›s war on Ukraine impacts the whole world' – Speech by the president of Ukraine to the Foreign Policy Community of Indonesia (FPC)', Office of the President of Ukraine] (27 May 2022).

'РНБО ініціює введення тимчасового керівництва на Укрзалізниці', *Українська правда* ['The NSDC appoints provisional management for the Ukrainian railways', *Ukrainska Pravda*] (30 July 2021).

Руденко, Анастасія, 'У цій країні можливо по-іншому', *День* [Rudenko, Anastasia, 'In this country, we can do things differently', *Den*] (24 November 2017).

'Секретар РНБО Олексій Данілов, Коли будуть санкції проти Коломойського', *Радіо НВ* ['NSDC secretary Oleksiy Danilov, when will there be new sanctions against Kolomoyskyi', *Radio NV*] (25 March 2021).

Сидоренко, Сергій, 'Лінас Лінкявічюс: Надто активна боротьба з Порошенком має не дуже добрий запах', *Європейська Правда* [Sydorenko, Serhiy, 'Linas Linkevičius: an overzealous prosecution of Poroshenko leaves a strange aftertaste', *Evropeiska Pravda*] (27 October 2020).

Сидоренко, Сергій, 'Забути все, окрім корупції: як Зеленський вичавив перемогу із саміту Україна-ЄС', *Європейська Правда* [Sydorenko, Serhiy, 'Forget everything but corruption: how Zelensky squeezed victory from the EU-Ukraine summit', *Evropeiska Pravda*] (7 October 2020).

Сидоренко, Сергій, 'Від "Зе" до Порошенка: що думають команди кандидатів про НАТО, ЄС, Донбас та реформи', *Європейська Правда* [Sydorenko, Serhiy, 'From "Ze" to Poroshenko: what the candidates think of NATO, the EU, the Donbas and reforms', *Evropeiska Pravda*] (25 February 2019).

'Скоро буду свистати, – Зеленський розповів, як почав вивчати українську мову', *24 Канал* ['Before long I'll be talking your ears off – Zelenksy tells how he has started learning Ukrainian', *Kanal 24*] (16 April 2017).

'Смолій: Я запитав у президента, чи повинен звільнитись, він відповів "так"', *Українська правда* ['Smoliy: I asked the president if I should step down, and he said "yes"', *Ukrainska Pravda*] (6 July 2020).

Спецпроект 'Квартал твоєї мрії', 1+1 [Special project 'The Kvartal of your dreams'] (16 March 2019).

'Суд зобов'язав фігуранта справи МН17 Цемаха не залишати місце постійного проживання в ОРДЛО', *Unian* ['Court orders MH17 suspect Tsemakh not to leave his home in Donetsk', *Unian*] (5 September 2019).

'США підтримали санкції України проти каналів Медведчука', *Європейська Правда* ['The United States support the Ukrainian sanctions against Medvedchuk's TV stations', *Evropeiska Pravda*] (3 February 2021).

'Суспільно-Політичні Настрої Населення: Листопад- Грудень 2018 Року', Київський міжнародний інститут соціології ['Socio-political attitudes of the population: November-December 2018', Kyiv International Institute of Sociology] (2018).

Тищенко, Катерина, 'В Україні може з' явитися 'промисловий ліс' – Данілов', *Українська правда* [Tyshchenko, Kateryna, 'An industrial forest may appear in Ukraine – Danilov', *Ukrainska Pravda*] (22 August 2021).

Тороп, Оксана, 'Олена Зеленська: "Після перемоги Вови хочу писати сценарії для 95 Кварталу"', *BBC News Україна* [Torop, Oksana, 'Olena Zelenska: "After Vova's victory, I want to be a writer for Kvartal 95"', *BBC News Ukraine*] (22 April 2019).

'У Києві з'явилися бігборди з Порошенком і Путіним', *LB.ua* ['Billboards with Poroshenko and Putin have appeared in Kyiv'] (9 April 2019).

Укази президента України № 43/2021, № 477/2021, № 268/2021, № 110/2021, Офіс Президента України [Decrees by the president of Ukraine nos. 43/2021, 268/2021, 110/2021, Office of the President of Ukraine] (2 February 2021, 20 September 2021, 24 June 2021, 23 March 2021).

Хоменко, Святослав , 'Олексій Данілов: план росіян був простий - знищення Зеленського', *BBC News Україна* [Khomenko, Shvatoslav, 'Oleksiy Danilov: the Russians' plan was simple – to kill Zelensky', *BBC News Ukraine*] (14 April 2022).

'Червона лінія. Корупція. Документальний фільм', *Українська правда* ['The red line. Corruption', *Ukrainska Pravda*] (15 December 2020).

'Чи варто Зеленському розпускати Раду та як змусити Путіна до зустрічі в нормандському форматі: інтерв'ю з амбасадоркою Німеччини', *ТСН* ['Whether Zelensky should dissolve the Rada, and how to force Putin to meet at the Normandy Format: interview with the German ambassador', *The TV-News*] (4 September 2021).

'Чому родина Зеленського проти того, аби він пішов на другий термін президентства', *Світське життя*, YouTube ['Why Zelensky's family objects to a second presidential term', *Lives of the Stars*, YouTube] (10 October 2021).

Шаталов, Денис, 'Місто кривого Рога. "Козацький міф" на локальному рівні: криворізький випадок.' Частина 1, *Historians* [Shatalov, Denys, 'The city of Krivoy Rog. The "Cossack myth" at local level: Kryvyi Rih.' Part 1] (3 June 2021).

Шаповал, Катерина '1993 рік. Гіперінфляція. Історія українського бізнесу', *Forbes* [Shapoval, Kateryna, 'The year 1993. Hyperinflation. The history of Ukrainian industry'] (6 July 2021).

'Що пообіцяв Байден Зеленському? Чого чекати від США? Відверто про переговори від Оксани Маркарової', *Європейська правда* ['What did Biden promise Zelensky? What can we expect from the US? Oksana Markarova speaks candidly about the negotiations', *Evropeiska Pravda*] (10 September 2021).

'Що Володимир Зеленський пише Олені Кравець?', *Зірковий шлях* ['What did Volodymyr Zelensky write to Olena Kravets?', *Star Trek*] (7 April 2022).

'Що відомо про батьків Зеленського: рідкісні сімейні фото', *РБК-Україна* ['What we know about Zelensky's parents: rare family photos', *RBK-Ukraina*] (4 April 2019).

'Я повний профан в економіці': у мережу злили прослушку наради Гончарука', *Українська правда* ['I'm an absolute layman when it comes to economics: Honcharuk's meeting leaked on the internet', *Ukrainska Pravda*] (15 January 2020).

Sources in Russian

'25 лет референдуму о сохранении СССР', Ельцин Центр, ['25 years since the referendum on the preservation of the Soviet Union', Yeltsin Centre] (17 March 2016).

'А. Руцкой считает, что Крым должен быть в составе России и подписать федеративный договор', *Интерфакс* ['A. Rutskoy believes that Crimea should be part of Russia and sign a federation agreement', *Interfax*] (4 April 1992).

'Артисты на дне рождения Януковича напели на \$330 тыс', *Росбалт* ['Artists appearing at Yanukovych's birthday earned 330,000 dollars', *Rosbalt*] (19 July 2011).

'Андрей Солдатов: Путину боятся рассказывать правду о войне', *Популярная Политика*, YouTube ['Andrei Soldatov: people are afraid to tell Putin the truth about the war', *Populyarnaya Politika*] (27 April 2022).

'Андрей Солдатов: в ФСБ ищут предателей', *Популярная Политика* ['Andrei Soldatov: the FSB is looking for traitors', *Populyarnaya Politika*] (8 April 2022).

'Алексей Гончарук', *В гостях у Дмитрия Гордона*, YouTube ['Oleksiy Honcharuk', *Live with Dmytro Hordon*] (July 2020).

'Андрей Богдан', *В гостях у Дмитрия Гордона*, YouTube ['Andriy Bohdan', *Live with Dmytro Hordon*] (July 2020).

Акименко, Александр, 'Самые громкие журналистские расследования, касающиеся украинского президента', *Insider* [Akimenko, Alexander, 'The most spectacular discoveries about the president of Ukraine'] (6 December 2013).

Богданов, Владимир, 'Говорит Москва, показывает Киев. Прямой эфир Путина на Украине собрал 80 тысяч вопросов', *Российская газета* [Bogdanov, Vladimir, 'Moscow speaks, Kyiv broadcasts. Live interview with Putin in Ukraine results in eighty thousand questions', *Rossiyskaya Gazeta*] (26 October 2004).

'Б. Ельцин и Л. Кравчук договорились приостановить действие своих указов по Черноморскому Флоту', *Интерфакс. Президентский вестник* ['B. Yelstin and L. Kravchuk agree to suspend their decrees on the Black-Sea Fleet', *Interfax. Presidential Bulletin*] (9 April 1992).

'Бандитский Кривбасс. Поименно', *Украина Криминальная* ['The criminal Kryvbas', *Ukraina Kriminalna*] (13 May 2004).

'Берите власть в свои руки! Нам с вами будет легче договориться, чем с этой шайкой наркоманов и неонацистов'. Путин призвал украинских военных устроить госпереворот', *Meduza* ['"Take power into your own hands! It will be easier to reach an agreement with you than with that pack of junkies and neo-Nazis." Putin calls on Ukrainian soldiers to stage a coup'] (25 February 2022).

'В России предложили завести уголовные дела против Зеленского и Роговцевой', *Гордон* ['Russia wanted to start criminal proceedings against Zelensky and Rogovtseva', *Hordon*] (7 February 2015).

'В 'Вечернем квартале' высмеяли памятник Ленину, 'Беркут' и российских журналистов', *TCH* [Vecherniy Kvartal jokes about Lenin statues, the Berkut and Russian journalists', *The TV-News*] (12 December 2013).

'В спецслужбах идут разговоры, что с Украиной что- то не так, и винят в этом Путина', *Радио Свобода* ['There is talk in the security services that things are not going well in Ukraine, and they blame Putin', *Radio Svoboda*] (18 May 2022).

'Вице-Президент России летит в Крым', *Интерфакс* ['Russian vice-president flies to Crimea', *Interfax*] (3 April 1992).

'Владимир Зеленский - серьезный шутник', *Cosmopolitan Ukraine* ['Volodymyr Zelensky is a real joker'] (March 2003).

'Владимир Зеленский крестил сына', *Главред* ['Zelensky christens his son', *Glavred*] (20 May 2013).

'Владимир Зеленский: 'Лицо украинского юмора должно успевать все', *Вечерний Томск* ['Volodymyr Zelensky: The face of Ukrainian comedy has everything within his reach', *Vecherniy Tomsk*] (29 November 2011).

'Владимир Зеленский', *В гостях у Дмитрия Гордона*, YouTube ['Volodymyr Zelensky', *Live with Dmytro Hordon*] (July 2018).

'Владимир Зеленский готовится к съемкам острой комедии с политическим оттенком. Съемки

40-серийной картины стартуют уже весной', *Комсомольская правда в Украине* ['Volodymyr Zelensky is preparing to shoot a hard-hitting comedy with political overtones. Shooting the 40-part series will start in the spring', *Komsomolskaya Pravda in Ukraïne*] (29 January 2015).

'Владимир Зеленский: Все имеющиеся деньги мы инвестируем в себя', *Amik.ru* ['Volodymyr Zelensky: I invest all the money I have in myself'] (11 December 2008).

'Владимир Зеленский больше не генеральный продюсер 'Интера', *Комсомольская правда в Украине* ['Volodymyr Zelensky is no longer general producer at Inter', *Komsomolskaya Pravda in Ukraïne*] (7 August 2011).

'Владимир Зеленский строит семейную идиллию в элитном клубном поселке', *ТСН* ['Volodymyr Zelensky builds his own family paradise in an elite closed community', *The TV-News*] (31 October 2013).

'Владимир Зеленский: от выступлений в переходах до 'Украинского квартала', *Наш Город* ['Volodymyr Zelensky: from performances in pedestrian underpasses to the Kvartal of Ukraine', *Nash Gorod*] (18 October 2010).

'Выборы президента 2004 года могут стать самыми грязными в истории независимой Украины - эксперты', *Интерфакс. Президентский вестник* ['The 2004 presidential elections could become the most sordid ever in independent Ukraine, experts say', *Interfax. Presidential Bulletin*] (10 December 2003).

Галаджий, Елена, Так что с миллиардом деревьев и институтом будущего? Как выполняют обещания Зеленского, *Комсомольская правда в Украине* [Haladzy, Olena, 'So how are things with the billion trees and the institute of the future? How Zelensky's promises are being implemented', *Komsomolskaya Pravda in Ukraine*] (21 September 2021).

Григорян, Анна, 'КВН для армян', *Планета Диаспора* [Grigorian, Anna, 'KVN for Armenians', *Planet of the Diaspora*] (2 September 2002).

'Дмитрий Разумков', *В гостях у Дмитрия Гордона*, YouTube [Dmytro Razumkov, *Live with Dmytro Hordon*] (January 2020).

'Евгений Кошевой', *В гостях у Дмитрия Гордона*, YouTube ['Yevhen Koshovy', *Live with Dmytro Hordon*] (November 2019).

'Евгений Кошевой', *Зе Интервьюер*, YouTube ['Yevhen Koshovy', *The Interviewer*] (31 August 2017).

Ельцин, Борис, *Записки президента: Размышления, воспоминания, впечатления* [Yeltsin, Boris, *Notes from a President. Reflections, Memories, Impressions.*] (Moscow 2008).

'Если кто-то у украинского народа что-то украл, он должен положить это на место'. Данилов пообещал, что СНБО не остановится на введенных санкциях', *Гордон* ['If someone steals something from the Ukrainian people, then they have to give it back. Danilov promises that the NSDC will not stop the current sanctions', *Hordon*] (19 February 2021).

Жарикова, Анна, 'Для своих я всегда зелёный', *Провинция* [Zharikova, Anna, 'For my own people I'm always green', *Provintsia*] (November 2002).

Жохова, Анастасия, 'Нешуточные деньги: как глава КВН зарабатывает на веселых и находчивых', *Forbes* [Zhokhova, Anastasia, 'Serious money: how the head of KVN turns a profit from the joyful and inventive'] (7 August 2013).

Жегулёв, Илья, 'Это не шутка, комик Владимир Зеленский — главный украинский политик', *Meduza* [Zhegulyov, Ilya, 'This is no joke: comic actor Zelensky is the most important Ukrainian politician'] (01 April 2019).

'За глаза. Владимир Зеленский', *Интер* ['Behind your back. Volodymyr Zelensky', *Inter*] (2010).

'Замгоссекретаря США: в войне в Украине убиты более 10 тысяч российских военных. Минобороны РФ сообщало о 1351 погибшем, *Current Time* ['US Under Secretary of State: over ten thousand Russian soldiers killed in the war in Ukraine. The Russian Ministry of Defence reports 1,351 deaths.'] (30 March 2022).

'Заявление Ельцина по Черноморскому Флоту', *Интерфакс* ['Yeltsin's statement on the Black Sea Fleet, *Interfax*] (3 April 1992).

'Зеленский любит холить женщин', *Блик* ['Zelensky likes to pamper women', *Blik*] (1 December 2008).

'Зеленский своим указом увеличил штат СНБО и обновил его структуру', *Гордон* ['With his order, Zelensky increases the staff complement of the NSDC and updates its structure', *Hordon*] (26 February 2021).

'Зеленский на Донбассе: Мы должны максимально шатать власть', *Spletni. biz* ['Zelensky in the Donbas: we must shake up power as much as possible'] (16 April 2014).

'Зеленский и команда придумали для 'Интера' 30 новых программ', *Комсомольская правда в Украине* ['Zelensky and his team think up thirty new programmes for Inter', *Komsomolskaya Pravda in Ukraine*] (27 December 2010).

'Зеленский: Буду ли еще баллотироваться? Подумаю. Одного срока недостаточно', *Гордон* ['Zelensky: Will I run for a second term? I'll think about it. One term is not enough', *Hordon*] (20 May 2020).

'Зеленский рассказал, как Янукович пытался закрыть Вечерний квартал', *Экономические известия* ['Zelensky tells of how Yanukovych tried to take *Vecherniy Kvartal* off the air', *Ekonomicheskie Izvestia*] (17 March 2014).

Зыгарь, Михаил, *Вся кремлевская рать. Краткая история современной России* [Zygar, Mikhail, *The Men of the Kremlin. A Short History of Contemporary Russia*] (Moscow, 2015).

'Исполнительная власть РФ делает все для успешного завершения процесса ратификации большого договора между Украиной и Россией - Посол РФ', *Интерфакс. Украина* ['The government of the Russian Federation is doing its utmost to finalise the ratification of the major treaty between Ukraine and Russia – Russian Ambassador', *Interfax Ukraina*] (15 January 1999).

Кабмин уволил Верланова и Нефьодова, *Ліга.net* ['The Cabinet sacks Verlanov and Nefodov', *Liga.net*] (24 April 2020).

Калинина Екатерина, 'Секрет '95-го квартала', *Московский Комсомолец в Кузбассе* [Kalinina, Jekatrina, 'The secret of Kvartal 95', *Moskovsky Komsomolets in the Kuzbas*] (October 2001).

'Как звезды шоу-бизнеса относятся к Евромайдану', *Дело* ['How showbiz stars feel about Euromaidan', *Delo*] (13 December 2013).

Касьянов, Георгий, *Украина 1991-2007: очерки новейшей истории* [Kasyanov, Georgiy, *Ukraine 1991-2007. Sketches of recent history*] (2008).

Квартал и его команда [The Kvartal Team, docuseries] (2014).

'Кабмин знает, что делать, но знать – недостаточно, нужно много работать', – Зеленский', *Фокус* ['The cabinet knows what to do, but knowing is not enough, we need to work, work, work', *Fokus*] (4 March 2020).

Кигурадзе, Темур, 'Чего ждет Майдан от *Петра* Порошенко?', *BBC News Русская служба* [Kiguradze, Temur, 'What Maidan expects from Petro Poroshenko', *BBC News Russian Service*] (26 May 2014).

'Коломойский запретил Зеленскому превращать Кернеса в мультперсонаж', *Korrespondent.eu* ['Kolomoyskyi refused to allow Zelensky to turn Kernes in a cartoon character'] (1 November 2013).

'Концерты Зеленского по определенным признакам можно считать формой 'гречкосейства', *Hromadske* ['Zelensky's performances can be seen as a form of bread and circuses'] (18 March 2019).

'Конец 'кнопкодавства' в Раде: почему сенсорную кнопку внедряли 13 лет', *Deutsche Welle* ['The end of push-buttons in the Rada: why touch sensors are being introduced after thirteen years'] (4 March 2021).

'Кто такой Денис Манжосов и почему возник скандал вокруг Зеленского', *24 Канал* ['Who is Denys

Manzhosov and why has a scandal emerged around Zelensky', *Kanal 24*]
(11 April 2019).

Крылова, Ольга, 'Владимир Зеленский одобряет служебные романы',
Регион 64 [Krylova, Olga, 'Volodymyr Zelensky approves of romances at
work', *Region 64*] (10 January 2013).

'Кравчук распорядился о передаче всех дислоцированных на Украине
воинских формирований под юрисдикцию Киева', *Интерфакс*
['Kravchuk orders all military units located in Ukraine to be transferred
to Ukrainian jurisdiction', *Interfax*] (5 April 1992).

Кучук, Марина, 'Депутаты подали свыше 16.000 правок к
'антиколомойскому' закону: список авторов', *Ліга.net* [Kuchuk,
Maryna, 'Delegates submit over 16,000 amendments to the "Anti-
Kolomoyskyi Bill"', *Liga.net*] (7 April 2020).

'Л.Кучма: никто не заявлял, что Украину хотят видеть в Европейском
Союзе', Финмаркет ['L. Kuchma: nobody has said they want to see
Ukraine in the EU', *Finmarket*] (1 October 2003).

'Алексей Гончарук', *В гостях у Дмитрия Гордона*, YouTube ['Leonid
Honcharuk', *Live with Dmytro Hordon*] (October 2016).

'Лидер движения "Держава" считает, что Совет Федерации не должен
ратифицировать договор между Россией и Украиной', *Интерфакс*
['The leader of "The State" party believes that the Federation Council
should not ratify the treaty between Russia and Ukraine', *Interfax*] (17
January 1999).

Лисицын, Николай, 'Зеленский и Вакарчук знают как объединить страну', *Комсомольская правда в Украине* [Lysytsyn, Nykola, 'Zelensky and Bakarchuk know how the country should be united', *Komsomolskaya Pravda in Ukraïne*] (18 April 2014).

Лисицын, Николай, 'Зеленский заявил, что Apple поможет Украине провести перепись населения в 2023 году', *Комсомольская правда в Украине* [Lysytsyn, Nykola, 'Zelensky announces that Apple will help Ukraine conduct census in 2023', *Komsomolskaya Pravda in Ukraïne*] (30 November 2021).

Мацегора, Екатерина, 'Все обещания Зеленского. Как новый президент будет изменять Украину', *Фокус* [Matseroga, Jetarina, 'All of Zelensky's promises. How the new president will change Ukraine', *Fokus*] (22 April 2019).

Мартынко, Кристина, 'Зеленский назвал покушение на Шефира 'ценой за преобразования', *Комсомольская правда в Украине* [Martynko, Krystyna, 'Zelensky labels the attack on Shefir as "the price of reform"', *Komsomolskaya Pravda in Ukraïne*] (23 September 2021).

Медведева, Наталия, 'Пошли против КСУ. Кабмин обязал НАПК немедленно восстановить доступ к реестру деклараций', *Ліга.net* [Medvedeva, Natalia, 'Attack on the Constitutional Court. The cabinet presses the NSDC to grant immediate access to the declaration register', *Liga.net*] (29 October 2020).

Медведева, Наталия, 'ЧВК Вагнера. Bellingcat снимает фильм о спецоперации, которую Зеленский отрицает', *Ліга.net* [Medvedeva, Natalia, 'The Paramilitary Wagner Group. Bellingcat is working on a documentary about the secret operation that Zelensky denies', *Liga.net*] (22 December 2022).

'Мнение знаменитостей о событиях в стране: 'После дождя всегда хорошая погода. Завтра все будет хорошо!', *Комсомольская правда в Украине* ['The opinions of famous people on events in the country: "After rain comes the sun. Tomorrow, will everything be OK!"', *Komsomolskaya Pravda in Ukraïne*] (20 February 2014).

Навольнева, Ирина, 'Так получилось. Как сериал 'Слуга народа' сделал шоумена и бизнесмена президентом Украины', *Hromadske* ['And so it was. How *Servant of the People* turned an actor and businessman into the president of Ukraine'] (18 June 2018).

'На какие вопросы об офшорах не ответил Зеленский. Рассказывает участница расследования 'Слідство. Інфо', *Current Time* ['Which questions about offshore holdings has Zelensky not answered? An investigator from Slidstvo.info tells'] (18 October 2021).

'Нацсовет не понял юмора', *Коммерсантъ Украина* ['The National Council did not understand the humour', *Kommersant Ukraina*] (20 January 2009).

Николаенко, Татьяна, 'Пришел, избрался, усидел? Правила президентства Петра Порошенко, *Ліга. net* [Nikolayenko, Tetyana, 'He came, he saw, he got re-elected. President Petro Porosjenko's rules of engagement', *Liga.net*] (2 February 2019).

Николаенко, Татьяна, 'Из шоумена в президенты за 90 дней, Правила блицкрига Владимира Зеленского', *Ліга.net* [Nikolayenko, Tetyana, 'From showman to president in 90 days. The rules of Volodymyr Zelensky's *Blitzkrieg*', *Liga.net*] (27 March 2019).

'Они смеялись за родину. Политический юмор стал в Украине очень востребованным продуктом', *Корреспондент.net* ['They laughed for their country. Political humour has become a sought-after commodity in Ukraine', *Korrespondent.net*] (24 January 2013).

'Он идет по жизни, смеясь', *Столица* ['He walks through life with laughter', *Stolitsa*] (17 June 2011).

'Офшоры Зеленского: у НАПК к декларации президента претензий нет', *Дело* ['Zelensky's offshore companies: the NSDC finds nothing suspect in the president's tax returns', *Delo*] (27 October 2021).

Перцев, Андрей, 'Довольных почти нет'. Как утверждают источники «Медузы», за три месяца Путин настроил против себя и 'партию войны', и тех, кто хочет мира. В Кремле надеются, что 'в обозримой перспективе' он уйдет, — и выбирают преемника, *Meduza* [Pertsev, *Andrei*, 'Almost nobody is satisfied. Meduza's sources confirm that over the previous three months, Putin has turned both the "war party" and those who want peace against him. The Kremlin hopes that he will step down soon and that a successor will be chosen.'] (24 May 2022).

'Передвиборча програма кандидата на пост Президента України Володимира Зеленського' ['The election programme for the Ukrainian presidency of Volodymyr Zelensky'] (2019).

'Под Минском задержаны 32 боевика иностранной частной военной компании', *Belta* ['32 foreign mercenaries apprehended close to Minsk'] (29 July 2020).

'Программы кандидатов: чем отличаются идеи Порошенко и Зеленского', *Deutsche Welle* ['The candidates' election platforms: how Poroshenko and Zelensky's ideas differ'] (11 April 2019).

Погуляевський, Марко, 'ЦИК официально объявила о победе Зеленского в выборах президента Украины', *Hromadske* [Pogulyaevsky, Marko, 'The Central Voting Agency reports Zelensky's victory in the Ukrainian presidential elections'] (30 April 2019).

'Подоляк: У Президента есть ряд инструментов, чтобы вернуть в нормальное русло ситуацию с КСУ', *Укринформ* ['Podolyak: the president has access to a whole range of instruments to ease the situation surrounding the Constitutional Court', *Ukrinform*] (29 October 2020).

'Порядочный, честный человек'. Гончарук в прощальной речи расхвалил президента', *Фокус* ['A normal, honest person. Honcharuk praises the president in his farewell speech', *Fokus*] (4 March 2020).

Путин, Владимир, 'Обращение Президента Российской Федерации' [Putin, Vladimir, 'Address by the president of the Russian Federation to the citizens of Russia'] (21 February 2022).

Путин, Владимир, 'Обращение Президента Российской Федерации' [Putin, Vladimir, 'Address to the citizens of Russia'] (24 February 2022).

Путин, Владимир, 'Об историческом единстве русских и украинцев', Администрация президента РФ [Putin, Vladimir 'On the historic unity of Russians and Ukrainians', website of the Administration of the President of the Russian Federation] (12 July 2021)

'Путин и Кучма договорятся о главном', *Российская газета* ['Putin and Kuchma reach agreement on key issues', *Rossiyskaya Gazeta*] (22 January 2004).

'Реакция командования Черноморского Флота на указ Кравчука о формировании на его основе Вмс тс Украины', *Интерфакс* ['Head of the Black Sea Fleet responds to Kravchuk's order to form the Ukrainian fleet on its basis', *Interfax*] (7 April 1992)

'Реакция Петра Порошенко на результаты первого экзит-пола', *НВ* ['Petro Poroshenko's response to the results of the first exit polls', *NV*] (21 April 2019).

'Редкий гость в семье Зеленских', *Наш Город* ['A rare guest in the Zelensky family', *Nash Gorod*] (22 October 2010).

'Рейтинги кандидатов в президенты Украины уже полгода остаются стабильными', *Интерфакс Новости Украины* ['The Ukrainian presidential candidate polls have remained stable for six months', *Interfax. News from Ukraine*] (16 January 2004).

Рейн, Настя, 'Правительство для людей'. Кто есть кто в новом Кабинете министров Украины', *Фокус* [Reyn, Nastya, 'The people's government. Who's who in Ukraine's ministerial cabinet', *Fokus*] (4 March 2020).

'Рябошапка о подозрении Порошенко: Это 'юридический трэш'. Но Венедиктова может его подписать', *Фокус* ['Riaboshapka on the suspected crimes of Poroshenko: "It was legal garbage. But perhaps Venediktova will sign off on it"', *Fokus*] (25 March 2020).

'СБУ засекретила расследование о прослушке Гончарука', *Фокус* ['SBU classifies the Honcharuk wiretap case', *Fokus*] (31 January 2020).

Скляренко, Диана, 'Шоу', *Крымская правда* [Sklyarenko, Diana, 'Show', *Krymskaya Pravda*] (8 August 2007).

Смирнов, Юрий & Шевчук, Сергей, 'Антиколомойский' закон: Зеленский и Порошенко – за, Коломойский и Тимошенко – против', *Ліга.net* [Smyrnov, Yuriy & Shevchuk, Serhiy, 'Zelensky and Poroshenko are in favour, Kolomoyskyi and Tymoshenko are against', *Liga.net*] (13 May 2020).

Смирнов, Юрий, 'Слуги народа. Кого Зеленский ведет в Раду: анализ кандидатов', *Ліга.net* [Smyrnov, Yuriy, 'Servant of the People. Who will Zelensky put in the Rada: an analysis of the candidates', *Liga.net*] (18 June 2019).

'СНБО хочет лишить 'Зеонбуд' монополии на рынке', *Гордон* ['The NSDC aims to deprive "Zeonbud" of a monopoly in the market', *Hordon*] (20 March 2021).

'Старый-добрый КВН или финансовая пирамида Маслякова', *Биржевой Лидер* ['Good-old KVN, or: Maslyakov's financial pyramid', *Birzhevoy Lider*] (8 August 2013).

Солдатов, Андрей & Бороган, Ирина, 'ГРУ выходит на первый план', *Agentura.ru* [Soldatov, Andrei & Borogan, Irina, 'De GRU steps into the foreground'] (9 May 2022).

Солдатов, Андрей & Бороган, Ирина, 'Путин начал чистки в разведке ФСБ', *Agentura.ru* [Soldatov, Andrei & Borogan, Irina, 'Putin starts to purge the intelligence department of the FSB'] (11 March 2022).

'Старые лица на главном', *Коммерсантъ Украина* ['Familiar faces take leadership', *Kommersant Ukraina*] (23 November 2011).

'Студия 'Квартал 95' заработала больше всех за год, а на пятки ей наступает 'Океан Эльзы', *Korrespondent. eu* ['Studio Kvartal 95 earned more in one year than Okean Elzy did in five'] (28 November 2013).

Софиенко, Наталия, 'Иск Приватбанка на \$5,5 млрд. Коломойского зовут на рассмотрение дела в Кипр', *Ліга.net* [Sofienko, Natalia, 'Kolomoyskyi summoned for a review of the Cyprus affair', *Liga.net*] (20 November 2021).

Софиенко, Наталия, 'Законопроект об олигархах внесен в Верховную Раду: основные положения', *Ліга.net* [Sofienko, Natalia, 'The Oligarchs' Bill has been submitted to the Verkhovna Rada: an overview', *Liga.net*] (3 June 2021).

Софиенко, Наталия, 'Шмыгаль заявил, что экономика Украины начала восстанавливаться после коронакризиса', *Ліга.net* [Sofienko, Natalia, 'Shmyhal announces that the economy is recovering after the COVID crisis', *Liga.net*] (2 February 2022).

Сысоев, Алексей, 'Владимир Зеленский: Если пойду в политику, 'Квартал' будет шутить надо мной еще похлеще', *Комсомольская правда в Украине* [Sysoyev, Oleksiy, 'Volodymyr Zelensky: "If I go into politics, Kvartal will make even harsher jokes about me"', *Komsomolskaya Pravda in Ukraïne*] (24 January 2018).

'США обеспокоены вмешательством административного ресурса в соревнования политических сил в Украине', *Интерфакс. Новости Украины* ['US concerned about interference of the president's office in the political battle in Ukraïne', *Interfax. News from Ukraine*] (04 December 2003).

Титко, Алиса, 'Для Донецка '95 квартал' подготовил специальные номера', *Комсомольская правда в Украине* [Tytko, Alysa, 'Kvartal 95 wrote special songs for Donetsk', *Komsomolskaya Pravda in Ukraïne*] (15 April 2014).

Тищенко, Марина, '8 марта - не день весны, а бездомный - не бомж: Елена Зеленская презентовала справочник безбарьерности', *Комсомольская правда в Украине* [Tishchenko, Maryna, '8 March is not Spring Day and homeless people are not "bums": Olena Zelensky presents her handbook on "open interaction"', *Komsomolskaya Pravda in Ukraïne*] (28 September 2021).

Ткаченко, Вера, 'Владимир Зеленский ('95 квартал'). Воин смеха' [Tkachenko, Vera, 'Volodymyr Zelensky (Kvartal 95), soldier of laughter'] (14 December 2008).

'Тухлый совок, – журналистка проехалась по "Сватах" и Зеленскому', *24 канал* ['"A bygone Soviet reality" – a journalist attacks "Svaty" and Zelensky', *Kanal 24*] (25 November 2017).

'Украинский фильм 'Любовь в большом городе' – в тройке лидеров по кассовым сборам в Украине в 2009 г.', *Интерфакс* ['Ukrainian film *Love in the Big City* reaches top 3 in the Ukrainian box office in 2009', *Interfax*] (13 April 2009).

'Фабрика смеха, Веселых и находчивых в Украине десятки тысяч, но только Владимир Зеленский научился шутить на миллионы долларов', *Forbes* ['The comedy factory: there are tens of thousands of joyful and inventive people in Ukraine, but only Zelensky knows how to make millions with his jokes.'] (January 2012).

'Фильм Любовь в большом городе вошел в тройку лидеров по кассовым сборам', *Корреспондент.net* ['*Love in the Big City* reaches box-office top-3', Korrespondent.net] (13 April 2009).

Филенко, Дмитрий, 'В Донецке Loboda покажет трюки, Олег Скрипка – линию одежды, а '95-й квартал' объединит страну, *Сегодня* [Fidenko, Dmyrto, 'In Donetsk, Loboda will perform tricks, Oleg Srkypka presents a clothing line, but Kvartal 95 will unite the country', *Segodnya*] (1 April 2014).

'ФСБ РФ: ответственный сотрудник ведомства находился в Киеве 20-21 февраля', *Интерфакс* ['FSB: a responsible officer was in Kyiv on 20 and 21 February', *Interfax*] (5 April 2014).

Халупа, Ирена, 'В Украине сатира возрождена, но это редкость на постсоветском пространстве', *Радио Азаттык* [Khalupa, Irena, 'Satire has emerged in Ukraine, but it is a rarity in the post-Soviet world', *Radio Azattyk*] (22 May 2009).

'Христо Грозев: 'В окружении Путина уже недовольны этой войной', *Популярная Политика*, YouTube ['Christo Grozev: "Everyone in Putin's circle is already unhappy about the war"', *Populyarnaya Politika*] (09 March 2022).

'Христо Грозев: 'В ФСБ будут чистки', *Популярная Политика*, YouTube ['Christo Grozev: there will be a clearout in the FSB ', *Populyarnaya Politika*] (13 March 2022).

Хоменко, Святослав, 'Как Леонид Кравчук спорил с Горбачевым, развалил СССР, а в конце прослезился', *BBC News Русская служба* [Khomenko, Sviatoslav, 'How Leonid Kravchuk took on Gorbachev, made the USSR collapse, and ultimately regretted it', *BBC News Russian Service*] (8 December 2021).

Хожателева, Юлия, 'Россияне призывают бойкотировать фильм с Зеленским, который называет жителей Донбасса мразями', *КП* [Khozhateleva, Yulia, 'Russians call to boycott the film starring Zelensky, whom the inhabitants of the Donbas called "scum"', KP] (11 October 2014).

'Что сможет Ющенко, если станет Богом? Эксклюзивное интервью с '95-м кварталом', *АТН* ['What will Yushchenko do if he becomes God? An exclusive interview with Kvartal 95', *ATN*] (15 December 2008).

'Что сказал Владимир Путин украинцам', *Коммерсантъ* ['What Putin told the Ukrainians', *Kommersant*] (26 October 2004).

Школьная, Анна, 'Интервью с Владимиром Зеленским 'Не со всеми президентами я был в хороших отношениях', *Сегодня* [Shkolnaya, Anna, 'Interview with Volodymyr Zelensky: "I did not get on well with all presidents"', *Segodnya*] (10 November 2015).

Школьная, Анна, 'Зеленский впервые прокомментировал скандал со снятием 'Квартала' с эфира', *Сегодня* [Shkolnaya, Anna, 'Zelensky comments for the first time on the scandal of Kvartal being taken off the air', *Segodnya*] (13 November 2015).

Школьная, Анна, 'Зеленский: 'Мы устали снимать в проектах российских звезд', *Like.lb.ua* [Shkolnaya, Anna, 'Zelensky: "We're sick of doing projects with Russian stars."'] (07 October 2013).

Щурко, Сергей, 'Владимир Зеленский: 'Не дай бог, Акиньшина была бы на нашей стороне…', *Pressball* [Shchurko, Sergey, 'Volodymyr Zelensky: God forbid that Akinshyna would be on our side'] (14 October 2014).

'Это война, которую нельзя проиграть – полный текст интервью Владимира и Елены Зеленских', *Свобода слова* ['This is a war that we must not lose. The full text of the interview with Volodymyr and Olena Zelensky', *Free Speech*] (21 May 2022).

Юдин, Денис, 'Показ фильма 'Офшор 95' о Зеленском хотели сорвать, но передумали', *Ліга.net* [Yudin, Denys, 'They wanted to cancel the screening of *Offshore 95*, but they changed their minds', *Liga.net*] (03 October 2021).

'Юрий Лужков: Почему нельзя подписывать договор с Украиной', *Московский комсомолец* ['Yuriy Luzhkov: why the treaty with Ukraine should not be signed', *Moskovsky Komsomolets*] (28 January 1999).

'Я понимаю, вы должны шутить, но иногда вы это делаете так по-свински'. Актер Великий прокомментировал 'обиды' Зеленского на 'Квартал 95', *Гордон* ['"I know that you guys need to make jokes, but sometimes they are pretty harsh", great actor comments on Zelensky's 'grievances' regarding Kvartal 95', *Hordon*] (9 November 2021).

'Янукович пожаловался Меркель на "очень сильную Россию"', *LB.ua* ['Yanukovych complained to Merkel about "a very strong Russia"'] (29 November 2013).

'Янукович и К⁰ за три года украли около $40 миллиардов – Петренко', *Укринформ* ['Petrenko: Yanukovych & co. stole around 40 billion dollars within three years', *Ukrinform*] (25 May 2017).

Other sources

Servant of the People, Party Conference on 2 October 2021, liveblog by the party.

Documentary: '*Sluha Narodu*. Postscriptum', YouTube (11 December 2015).

Joint press conference on the outcomes of a meeting during the Normandy Format, website of the Office of the President of the Russian Federation (9 December 2019).

Kvartal 95, shows in Ukraine and Russia, YouTube (1999-2003).

Podolyak, Mychailo, Facebook post (13 February 2021).

Putin, Vladimir, press conference on 4 March, website of the Office of the President of the Russian Federation.

Poroshenko, Petro, 'Speech to the nation', Facebook (18 April 2021).

Sluha Narodu [Servant of the People], Season 1, YouTube (2016).

Sternenko, Serhiy, Telegram post (18 February 2022).

Ukrainian armed forces, posts on Facebook and own website.

Reviews by fans of Volodymyr Zelensky, kvartal95. narod.ru via archive.org (2002-2004).

Vecherniy Kvartal, television broadcasts (2004-2022).

Zelensky, Volodymyr, posts on Twitter, Facebook,

Instagram and Telegram (2017-2022).

'Engrossing and frankly deeply troubling...
'Former senior British diplomat Snell explains how Britain's often
incompetent, inconsistent and sometimes downright greedy
foreign policy has [made] the world a more dangerous place.'

Caroline Sanderson,
Editor's Choice,
The Bookseller

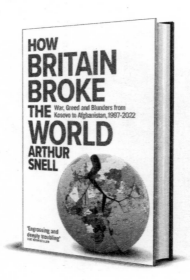

ISBN 9781912454600 (hardback, £25)
ISBN 9781912454617 (ebook, £15.99)

HOW BRITAIN BROKE THE WORLD
War, Greed and Blunders from Kosovo
to Afghanistan, 1997-2022
Arthur Snell
416 pages
History/Politics